THE CAREER IDEAS FOR KIDS SERIES

Second Edition

DIANE LINDSEY REEVES

with
LINDSEY CLASEN

Illustrations by
NANCY BOND

Ferguson
An imprint of Infobase Publishing

CAREER IDEAS FOR KIDS WHO LIKE TALKING, Second Edition

Copyright © 2007, 1998 by Diane Lindsey Reeves

Ferguson
An imprint of Infobase Publishing
132 West 31st Street
New York NY 10001

Library of Congress Cataloging-in-Publication Data
Reeves, Diane Lindsey, 1959-
   Career ideas for kids who like talking / Diane Lindsey Reeves with Lindsey Clasen ; illustrations by Nancy Bond. — 2nd ed.
      p. cm. — (The career ideas for kids series)
   Rev. ed. of: Talking. c1998.
   Includes bibliographical references and index.
   ISBN-13: 978-0-8160-6553-0 (hardcover : alk. paper)
   ISBN-10: 0-8160-6553-5 (hardcover : alk. paper) 1. Vocational guidance—Juvenile literature. 2. Occupations—Juvenile literature. 3. Professions—Juvenile literature. 4. Mass media—Vocational guidance—Juvenile literature. I. Clasen, Lindsey. II. Reeves, Diane Lindsey, 1959- Talking. III. Title.
   HF5381.2.R43 2007
   331.702—dc22   2007002935

Ferguson books are available at special discounts when purchased in bulk quantities for businesses, associations, institutions, or sales promotions. Please call our Special Sales Department in New York at (212) 967-8800 or (800) 322-8755.

You can find Ferguson on the World Wide Web at http://www.fergpubco.com

Original text and cover design by Smart Graphics
Illustrations by Nancy Bond

Printed in the United States of America

MP Hermitage 10 9 8 7 6 5 4 3 2 1

CONTENTS

ACKNOWLEDGMENTS

A million thanks to the people who took the time to share their career stories and provide photos for this book:

Deborah Alexander
Lori Fentem
Rose Forbes
Robert Gelinas
Lori Hurd
Jerome Jewell
Peter Jones
Mark Miller
Scott Moore
Gregory Mueller
Diana Nelson
Michaelanne Roberts
Gail S. Schoettler
Carrie Sherr
Rita Tateel

Finally, much appreciation and admiration is due to all the behind-the-scenes people at Ferguson who have done so much to make this series all that it is. With extra thanks to James Chambers and Sarah Fogarty.

MAKE A CHOICE!

Choices.

You make them every day. What do I want for breakfast? Which shirt can I pull out of the dirty-clothes hamper to wear to school today? Should I finish my homework or play video games?

Some choices don't make much difference in the overall scheme of things. Face it; who really cares whether you wear the blue shirt or the red one?

Other choices are a major big deal. Figuring out what you want to be when you grow up is one of those all-important choices.

But, you say, you're just a kid. How are you supposed to know what you want to do with your life?

You're right: 10, 11, 12, and even 13 are a bit young to know exactly what and where and how you're going to do whatever it is you're going to do as an adult. But it's the perfect time to start making some important discoveries about who you are, what you like to do, and what you do best. It's a great time to start exploring the options and experimenting with different ideas. In fact, there's never a better time to mess around with different career ideas without messing up your life.

When it comes to picking a career, you've basically got two choices.

CHOICE A

You can be like lots of other people and just go with the flow. Float through school doing only what you absolutely have to in order to graduate, take any job you can find, collect a paycheck, and meander your way to retirement without making much of a splash in life.

Although many people take this route and do just fine, others end up settling for second best. They miss out on a meaningful education, satisfying work, and the rewards of a focused and well-planned career. That's why this path is not an especially good idea for someone who actually wants to have a life.

CHOICE B

Other people get a little more involved in choosing a career. They figure out what they want to accomplish in their lives— whether it's making a difference, making lots of money, or simply enjoying what they do. Then they find out what it takes to reach that goal, and set about doing it with gusto. It's kind of like these people do things on purpose instead of letting life happen by accident.

Choosing A is like going to an ice cream parlor where there are all kinds of awesome flavors and ordering a single scoop of plain vanilla. Going with Choice B is more like visiting that same ice cream parlor and ordering a super duper brownie sundae drizzled with hot fudge, smothered in whip cream, and topped with a big red cherry.

Do you see the difference?

Reading this book is a great idea for kids who want to go after life in a big way. It provides a first step toward learning about careers that match your skills, values, and dreams. It will help you make the most out of your time in school and maybe even inspire you to—as the U.S. Army so proudly says—"be all that you can be."

Ready for the challenge of Choice B? If so, read the next section for instructions on how to get started.

HOW TO USE THIS BOOK

This book isn't just about interesting careers that other people have. It's also a book about interesting careers that you can have.

Of course, it won't do you a bit of good to just read this book. To get the whole shebang, you're going to have to jump in with both feet, roll up your sleeves, put on your thinking cap—whatever it takes—to help you do these three things:

- ☀ Discover what you do best and enjoy the most. (This is the secret ingredient for finding work that's perfect for you.)

☼ Explore ways to match your interests and abilities with career ideas.
☼ Experiment with lots of different ideas until you find the ideal career. (It's like trying on all kinds of hats to see which ones fit!)

Use this book as a road map to some exciting career destinations. Here's what to expect in the chapters that follow.

GET IN GEAR!

First stop: discover. These activities will help you uncover important clues about the special traits and abilities that make you *you*. When you are finished you will have developed a personal Skill Set that will help guide you to career ideas in the next chapter.

TAKE A TRIP!

Next stop: explore. Cruise down the career idea highway and find out about a variety of career ideas that are especially appropriate for people who like talking. Use the Skill Set chart at the beginning of each career profile to match your own interests with those required for success on the job.

Once you've identified a career that interests you, kick your exploration into high gear by checking out some of the Web sites, library resources, and professional organizations listed at the end of each career profile. For an extra challenge, follow the instructions for the Try It Out activities.

MAKE A VERBAL DETOUR!

Here's your chance to explore up-and-coming opportunities in communications as well as the tried-and-true fields of writing and teaching.

Just when you thought you'd seen it all, here come dozens of interesting talking ideas to add to the career mix. Charge

up your career search by learning all you can about some of these opportunities.

DON'T STOP NOW!

Third stop: experiment. The library, the telephone, a computer, and a mentor—four keys to a successful career planning adventure. Use them well, and before long you'll be on the trail of some hot career ideas of your own.

WHAT'S NEXT?

Make a plan! Chart your course (or at least the next stop) with these career planning road maps. Whether you're moving full steam ahead with a great idea or get slowed down at a yellow light of indecision, these road maps will keep you moving forward toward a great future.

Use a pencil—you're bound to make a detour or two along the way. But, hey, you've got to start somewhere.

HOORAY! YOU DID IT!

Some final rules of the road before sending you off to new adventures.

SOME FUTURE DESTINATIONS

This section lists a few career planning tools you'll want to know about.

You've got a lot of ground to cover in this phase of your career planning journey. Start your engines and get ready for an exciting adventure!

GET IN GEAR!

Career planning is a lifelong journey. There's usually more than one way to get where you're going, and there are often some interesting detours along the way. But you have to start somewhere. So rev up and find out all you can about one-of-a-kind, specially designed you. That's the first stop on what can be the most exciting trip of your life!

To get started, complete the five exercises described throughout the following pages.

DISCOVER #1: WATCH FOR SIGNS ALONG THE WAY

Road signs help drivers figure out how to get where they want to go. They provide clues about direction, road conditions, and safety. Your career road signs will provide clues about who you are, what you like, and what you do best. These clues can help you decide where to look for the career ideas that are best for you.

Complete the following statements to make them true for you. There are no right or wrong answers. Jot down the response that describes you best. Your answers will provide important clues about career paths you should explore.

Please Note: If this book does not belong to you, write your responses on a separate sheet of paper.

On my last report card, I got the best grade in _____ .

On my last report card, I got the worst grade in _____ .

I am happiest when _____ .

Something I can do for hours without getting bored is _____ .

Something that bores me out of my mind is _____ .

My favorite class is _____ .

My least favorite class is _____ .

The one thing I'd like to accomplish with my life is _____ .

My favorite thing to do after school is

_____ .

My least favorite thing to do after school is _____ .

Something I'm really good at is _____ .

Something really tough for me to do is _____ .

My favorite adult person is _____

because _____ .

When I grow up _____ .

The kinds of books I like to read are about _____ .

The kinds of videos I like to watch are about _____ .

DISCOVER #2: RULES OF THE ROAD

Pretty much any job you can think of involves six common ingredients. Whether the work requires saving the world or selling bananas, all work revolves around a central **purpose** or reason for existing. All work is conducted somewhere, in some **place**, whether it's on the 28th floor of a city sky-scraper or on a cruise ship in the middle of an ocean. All work requires a certain **time** commitment and is performed using various types of **tools**. **People** also play an important part in most jobs—whether the job involves interacting with lots or very few of them. And, especially from where you are sitting as a kid still in school, all work involves some type of **preparation** to learn how to do the job.

Another word for these six common ingredients is "values." Each one represents important aspects of work that people value in different ways. The following activity will give you a chance to think about what matters most to you in each of these areas. That way you'll get a better idea of things to look for as you explore different careers.

Here's how the process works:

First, read the statements listed for each value on the following pages. Decide which, if any, represent your idea of an ideal job.

Next, take a look at the grid on page 16. For every value statement with which you agreed, draw its symbol in the appropriate space on your grid. (If this book doesn't belong to you, use a blank sheet of paper to draw your own grid with six big spaces.) Or, if you want to get really fancy, cut pictures out of magazines and glue them into the appropriate space. If you do not see a symbol that represents your best answer, make up a new one and sketch it in the appropriate box.

When you are finished, you'll have a very useful picture of the kinds of values that matter most to you in your future job.

PURPOSE

Which of the following statements describes what you most hope to accomplish in your future work? Pick as many as are true for you and feel free to add others.

♥	❏	I want to help other people.
	❏	I want to make lots of money.
★	❏	I want to do something I really believe in.
	❏	I want to make things.
	❏	I want to use my brain power in challenging ways.
	❏	I want to work with my own creative ideas.
	❏	I want to be very successful.
	❏	I want to find a good company and stick with it for the rest of my life.
	❏	I want to be famous.

Other purpose-related things that are especially important to me are

		PLACE
		When you think about your future work, what kind of place would you most like to do it in? Pick as many as are true for you and feel free to add others.

	❏	I want to work in a big city skyscraper.
	❏	I want to work in a shopping mall or retail store.
	❏	I want to work in the great outdoors.
	❏	I want to travel a lot for my work.
	❏	I want to work out of my own home.
	❏	I want to work for a government agency.
	❏	I want to work in a school or university.
	❏	I want to work in a factory or laboratory.

Other place-related things that are especially important to me are

GET IN GEAR!

TIME When you think about your future work, what kind of schedule sounds most appealing to you? Pick as many as are true for you and feel free to add others.		
	❏	I'd rather work regular business hours—nine to five, Monday through Friday.
	❏	I'd like to have lots of vacation time.
	❏	I'd prefer a flexible schedule so I can balance my work, family, and personal needs.
	❏	I'd like to work nights only so my days are free.
	❏	I'd like to work where the pace is fast and I stay busy all day.
	❏	I'd like to work where I would always know exactly what I'm supposed to do.
	❏	I'd like to work where I could plan my own day.
	❏	I'd like to work where there's lots of variety and no two days are alike.

Other time-related things that are especially important to me are

TOOLS

What kinds of things would you most like to work with? Pick as many as are true for you and feel free to add others.

👤	❏	I'd prefer to work mostly with people.
💻	❏	I'd prefer to work mostly with technology.
🔩	❏	I'd prefer to work mostly with machines.
🛍️	❏	I'd prefer to work mostly with products people buy.
✈️	❏	I'd prefer to work mostly with planes, trains, automobiles, or other things that go.
🧠	❏	I'd prefer to work mostly with ideas.
📖	❏	I'd prefer to work mostly with information.
🌳	❏	I'd prefer to work mostly with nature.

Other tool-related things that are especially important to me are

PEOPLE

What role do other people play in your future work? How many do you want to interact with on a daily basis? What age group would you most enjoy working with? Pick as many as are true for you and feel free to add others.

	❏	I'd like to work with lots of people all day long.
	❏	I'd prefer to work alone most of the time.
	❏	I'd like to work as part of a team.
	❏	I'd like to work with people I might choose as friends.
	❏	I'd like to work with babies, children, or teenagers,
	❏	I'd like to work mostly with elderly people.
	❏	I'd like to work mostly with people who are in trouble.
	❏	I'd like to work mostly with people who are ill.

Other people-related things that are especially important to me are

PREPARATION

When you think about your future work, how much time and energy do you want to devote to preparing for it? Pick as many as are true for you and feel free to add others.

	❏	I want to find a job that requires a college degree.
	❏	I want to find a job where I could learn what I need to know on the job.
	❏	I want to find a job that requires no additional training after I graduate from high school.
	❏	I want to find a job where the more education I get, the better my chances for a better job.
	❏	I want to run my own business and be my own boss.

Other preparation-related things that are especially important to me are

Now that you've uncovered some word clues about the types of values that are most important to you, use the grid on the following page (or use a separate sheet of paper if this book does not belong to you) to "paint a picture" of your ideal future career. Use the icons as ideas for how to visualize each statement. Or, if you'd like to get really creative, get a large sheet of paper, some markers, magazines, and glue or tape and create a collage.

PURPOSE	PLACE	TIME
TOOLS	**PEOPLE**	**PREPARATION**

DISCOVER #3: DANGEROUS DETOURS

Half of figuring out what you do want to do is figuring out what you don't want to do. Get a jump start on this process by making a list of 10 careers you already know you absolutely don't want to do.

Warning: Failure to heed early warnings signs to avoid careers like this can result in long hours of boredom and frustration spent doing a job you just weren't meant to do.

(If this book does not belong to you, make your list on a separate sheet of paper.)

1. _____   _____
2. _____   _____
3. _____   _____

4. _____   _____

5. _____   _____

6. _____   _____

7. _____   _____

8. _____   _____

9. _____   _____

10. _____   _____

Red Flag Summary:
Look over your list, and in the second column above (or on a separate sheet of paper) see if you can summarize what it is about these jobs that makes you want to avoid them like a bad case of cooties.

DISCOVER #4: ULTIMATE CAREER DESTINATION

Imagine that your dream job is like a favorite tourist destination, and you have to convince other people to pick it over every other career in the world. How would you describe it? What features make it especially appealing to you? What does a person have to do to have a career like it?

Take a blank sheet of paper and fold it into thirds. Fill each column on both sides with words and pictures that create a vivid image of what you'd most like your future career to be.

Special note: Just for now, instead of actually naming a specific career, describe what your ideal career would be like. In places where the name of the career would be used, leave a blank space like this _____. For instance: For people who want to become rich and famous, being a _____ is the way to go.

DISCOVER #5: GET SOME DIRECTION

It's easy to get lost when you don't have a good idea of where you want to go. This is especially true when you start thinking about what to do with the rest of your life. Unless you focus on where you want to go, you might get lost or even miss the exit. This discover exercise will help you connect your own interests and abilities with a whole world of career opportunities.

Mark the activities that you enjoy doing or would enjoy doing if you had the chance. Be picky. Don't mark ideas that you wish you would do. Mark only those that you would really do. For instance, if skydiving sounds appealing but you'd never do it because you are terrified of heights, don't mark it.

Please Note: If this book does not belong to you, write your responses on a separate sheet of paper.

- ❏ 1. Rescue a cat stuck in a tree
- ❏ 2. Paint a mural on the cafeteria wall
- ❏ 3. Run for student council
- ❏ 4. Send e-mail to a "pen pal" in another state
- ❏ 5. Find out all there is to know about the American Revolution
- ❏ 6. Survey your classmates to find out what they do after school
- ❏ 7. Try out for the school play
- ❏ 8. Dissect a frog and identify the different organs
- ❏ 9. Play baseball, soccer, football, or _____ (fill in your favorite sport)

❏ 10. Talk on the phone to just about anyone who will talk back

❏ 11. Try foods from all over the world—Thailand, Poland, Japan, etc.

❏ 12. Write poems about things that are happening in your life

❏ 13. Create a really scary haunted house to take your friends through on Halloween

❏ 14. Bake a cake and decorate it for your best friend's birthday

❏ 15. Sell enough advertisements for the school yearbook to win a trip to Walt Disney World

❏ 16. Simulate an imaginary flight through space on your computer screen

❏ 17. Collect stamps, coins, baseball cards, or whatever and organize them into a fancy display

❏ 18. Build model airplanes, boats, doll houses, or anything from kits

❏ 19. Teach your friends a new dance routine

❏ 20. Watch the stars come out at night and see how many constellations you can find

❏ 21. Watch baseball, soccer, football, or _____ (fill in your favorite sport) on TV

❏ 22. Give a speech in front of the entire school

❏ 23. Plan the class field trip to Washington, D.C.

❏ 24. Read everything in sight, including the back of the cereal box

❏ 25. Figure out "who dunnit" in a mystery story

❏ 26. Make a poster announcing the school football game

❏ 27. Think up a new way to make the lunch line move faster and explain it to the cafeteria staff

❏ 28. Put together a multimedia show for a school assembly using music and lots of pictures and graphics

❏ 29. Visit historic landmarks like the Statue of Liberty and Civil War battlegrounds

❏ 30. Invest your allowance in the stock market and keep track of how it does

❏ 31. Go to the ballet or opera every time you get the chance

❑ 32. Do experiments with a chemistry set

❑ 33. Keep score at your sister's Little League game

❑ 34. Use lots of funny voices when reading stories to children

❑ 35. Ride on airplanes, trains, boats—anything that moves

❑ 36. Interview the new exchange student for an article in the school newspaper

❑ 37. Build your own treehouse

❑ 38. Visit an art museum and pick out your favorite painting

❑ 39. Play Monopoly in an all-night championship challenge

❑ 40. Make a chart on the computer to show how much soda students buy from the school vending machines each week

❑ 41. Find out all you can about your family ancestors and make a family tree

❑ 42. Keep track of how much your team earns to buy new uniforms

❑ 43. Play an instrument in the school band or orchestra

❑ 44. Take things apart and put them back together again

❑ 45. Write stories about sports for the school newspaper

❑ 46. Listen to other people talk about their problems
❑ 47. Imagine yourself in exotic places
❑ 48. Hang around bookstores and libraries
❑ 49. Play harmless practical jokes on April Fools' Day
❑ 50. Take photographs at the school talent show
❑ 51. Make money by setting up your own business— paper route, lemonade stand, etc.
❑ 52. Create an imaginary city using a computer
❑ 53. Look for Native American artifacts and arrowheads
❑ 54. Do 3-D puzzles
❑ 55. Keep track of the top 10 songs of the week
❑ 56. Read about famous inventors and their inventions
❑ 57. Make play-by-play announcements at the school football game
❑ 58. Answer the phones during a telethon to raise money for orphans
❑ 59. Be an exchange student in another country
❑ 60. Write down all your secret thoughts and favorite sayings in a journal
❑ 61. Jump out of an airplane (with a parachute, of course)
❑ 62. Use a video camera to make your own movies
❑ 63. Get your friends together to help clean up your town after a hurricane

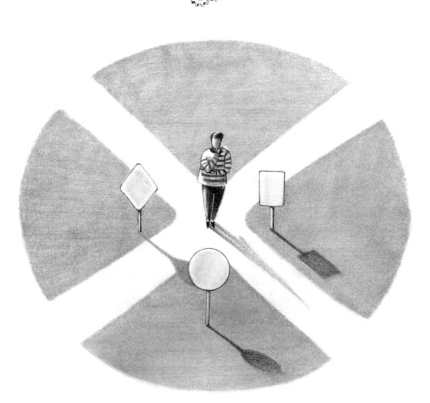

❏ 64. Spend your summer at a computer camp learning lots of new computer programs

❏ 65. Help your little brother or sister make ink out of blueberry juice

❏ 66. Build bridges, skyscrapers, and other structures out of LEGOs

❏ 67. Plan a concert in the park for little kids

❏ 68. Collect different kinds of rocks

❏ 69. Help plan a sports tournament

❏ 70. Be DJ for the school dance

❏ 71. Learn how to fly a plane or sail a boat

❏ 72. Write funny captions for pictures in the school yearbook

❏ 73. Scuba dive to search for buried treasure

❏ 74. Sketch pictures of your friends

❏ 75. Pick out neat stuff to sell at the school store

❏ 76. Answer your classmates' questions about how to use the computer

❏ 77. Make a timeline showing important things that happened during the year

❏ 78. Draw a map showing how to get to your house from school

❏ 79. Make up new words to your favorite songs

❏ 80. Take a hike and name the different kinds of trees, birds, or flowers

❏ 81. Referee intramural basketball games

❏ 82. Join the school debate team

❏ 83. Make a poster with postcards from all the places you went on your summer vacation

❏ 84. Write down stories that your grandparents tell you about when they were young

CALCULATE THE CLUES

Now is your chance to add it all up. Each of the 12 boxes on the following pages contains an interest area that is common to both your world and the world of work. Follow these directions to discover your personal Skill Set:

1. Find all of the numbers that you checked on pages 18–23 in the following boxes and mark them

with an X. Work your way all the way through number 84.

2. Go back and count the Xs marked for each interest area. Write that number in the space that says "Total."

3. Find the interest area with the highest total and put a number one in the "Rank" blank of that box. Repeat this process for the next two highest scoring areas. Rank the second highest as number two and the third highest as number three.

4. If you have more than three strong areas, choose the three that are most important and interesting to you.

Remember: If this book does not belong to you, write your responses on a separate sheet of paper.

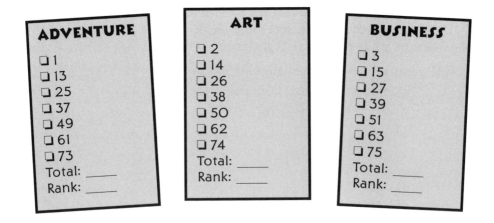

ADVENTURE

❑ 1
❑ 13
❑ 25
❑ 37
❑ 49
❑ 61
❑ 73
Total: _____
Rank: _____

ART

❑ 2
❑ 14
❑ 26
❑ 38
❑ 50
❑ 62
❑ 74
Total: _____
Rank: _____

BUSINESS

❑ 3
❑ 15
❑ 27
❑ 39
❑ 51
❑ 63
❑ 75
Total: _____
Rank: _____

GET IN GEAR!

COMPUTERS
- [ ] 4
- [ ] 16
- [ ] 28
- [ ] 40
- [ ] 52
- [ ] 64
- [ ] 76
Total: _____
Rank: _____

HISTORY
- [ ] 5
- [ ] 17
- [ ] 29
- [ ] 41
- [ ] 53
- [ ] 65
- [ ] 77
Total: _____
Rank: _____

MATH
- [ ] 6
- [ ] 18
- [ ] 30
- [ ] 42
- [ ] 54
- [ ] 66
- [ ] 78
Total: _____
Rank: _____

MUSIC/DANCE
- [ ] 7
- [ ] 19
- [ ] 31
- [ ] 43
- [ ] 55
- [ ] 67
- [ ] 79
Total: _____
Rank: _____

SCIENCE
- [ ] 8
- [ ] 20
- [ ] 32
- [ ] 44
- [ ] 56
- [ ] 68
- [ ] 80
Total: _____
Rank: _____

SPORTS
- [ ] 9
- [ ] 21
- [ ] 33
- [ ] 45
- [ ] 57
- [ ] 69
- [ ] 81
Total: _____
Rank: _____

TALKING
- [ ] 10
- [ ] 22
- [ ] 34
- [ ] 46
- [ ] 58
- [ ] 70
- [ ] 82
Total: _____
Rank: _____

TRAVEL
- [ ] 11
- [ ] 23
- [ ] 35
- [ ] 47
- [ ] 59
- [ ] 71
- [ ] 83
Total: _____
Rank: _____

WRITING
- [ ] 12
- [ ] 24
- [ ] 36
- [ ] 48
- [ ] 60
- [ ] 72
- [ ] 84
Total: _____
Rank: _____

What are your top three interest areas? List them here (or on a separate piece of paper).

1. _____

2. _____

3. _____

This is your personal Skill Set and provides important clues about the kinds of work you're most likely to enjoy. Remember it and look for career ideas with a Skill Set that matches yours most closely. You'll find a Skill Set box at the beginning of each career profile in the following section.

TAKE A TRIP!

Cruise down the career idea highway and enjoy in-depth profiles of some of the interesting options in this field. Keep in mind all that you've discovered about yourself so far. Find the careers that match your own Skill Set first. Then keep considering the other ideas—exploration is the name of this game.

Talking careers are based on exceptionally good communication skills. Keep in mind that communication skills are a two-way street with talking going one way and listening coming back. Good communicators can't have one skill without the other. They're a natural pair—sort of like shoes and socks.

As you browse through the following talking career ideas, you may be surprised to discover that many communication careers share two common denominators. First, communicators of all kinds use computers. Talkers—whether on the phone, the radio, the television, or in person—rely heavily on information and need a way to keep track of it.

The second common denominator is that talkers like people. Their jobs often require that they spend lots of time with people, so it really helps if they actually like the people they are working with.

Talking careers open up a wide variety of options. Some careers require college; some don't. Some careers can be done with just a little bit of training on the job; others require extensive training. Most of all, these careers require you to have fun while you talk.

As you read about the following careers, imagine yourself doing each job and ask yourself the following questions:

- ☀ Would I like it?
- ☀ Would I be good at it?
- ☀ Is it the stuff my career dreams are made of?

If so, make a quick exit to explore what it involves, try it out, check it out, and get acquainted. Look out for the symbols below.

Buckle up and enjoy the trip!

 TRY IT OUT

 CHECK IT OUT

🖱 ON THE WEB

📚 AT THE LIBRARY

🗣 WITH THE EXPERTS

A NOTE ON WEB SITES
Internet sites tend to move around the Web a bit. If you have trouble finding a particular site, use an Internet browser to find a specific Web site or type of information.

Air Traffic Controller

WHAT IS AN AIR TRAFFIC CONTROLLER?

Picture a police officer directing traffic. Hold that thought and replace the well-marked streets with huge runways and the big, blue, wide-open sky. That, in a nutshell, is what air traffic controllers do. They are responsible for keeping planes a safe distance from each other, both in the air and on the ground at the airport. They help pilots keep on course during flight and route them in the safest way possible. Assuring happy and safe takeoffs and landings is their number-one concern.

Another way to visualize this demanding profession is to think of a juggler keeping several balls in the air at once. It's the same concept for an air traffic controller, except that instead of harmless rubber balls, they are juggling several airplanes full of people and other precious cargo. Efficiency, organization, competency, and total concentration are key attributes that contribute to getting planes and people where they need to be—on time.

Additionally, air traffic controllers must stay in top physical and mental shape to withstand the stresses and demands of the job. They must possess good communication skills and must be able to speak in clear, distinct voices. With so many planes coming and going, the ability to think fast, coupled with exceptional decision-making skills, is an absolute must.

There are three types of controllers. One controller, the **enroute controller**, keeps in touch with planes while they are between airports. These controllers work in one of 24 special centers across the country in locations away from airports. They make sure planes stay in their "lanes" while they are flying at altitudes at or above 17,000 feet. The typical center is responsible for more than 100,000 square miles of airspace.

Another controller, called the **terminal controller**, directs traffic while planes approach, take off, and land at his or her airport. They generally control air traffic flying below 17,000 feet within about 20 miles of the airport. They work in the control towers and radar control rooms.

The **tower controller**, the third type of controller, makes sure that pilots flying within 5 to 10 miles of the airport have all the information they need for a safe flight. The tower controller provides information about weather and current airport conditions that might affect takeoffs and landings. These controllers must often provide advice based on their own observations and experience.

All controllers use radar and other high-tech equipment to do their jobs. Computers play a big part in helping controllers keep planes on course and on schedule. All controllers also work under fairly stressful conditions in a high-energy environment. And one other common ingredient is shared by all types of controllers: There is no room for mistakes!

To become an air traffic controller you must take lots of tests both before you get the job and after. College is not a must, but you will need to have some work experience. Aptitude exams must be passed. There are some age limitations as well. Top physical condition and mental readiness are key requirements. Candidates must be free of anything that could keep them from performing at their best day after day; no drugs or alcohol are allowed here!

Trainees go through the Federal Aviation Administration Academy in Oklahoma. There they learn about the regulations, the equipment, and how planes fly. They also gain experience in a simulated control tower environment. Once the training is completed, trainees must pass another test before officially qualifying as air traffic controllers.

It isn't an easy job, but air traffic controllers are a vital link in keeping the skies safe and bringing the world closer together.

☞ TRY IT OUT

AIRPORT IN A BOX

Construct a model of your idea of a model airport. Cut the sides of a large box down to a height of about six inches and use poster board and markers to define the space. Use graph paper to sketch out the elements. Some important considerations: How large is the airport? How many runways does it have? Do those runways go north and south or east and west? Why do they face the way they do?

✔ CHECK IT OUT

🖱 ON THE WEB

"CONTROL TOWER, THIS IS..."

The Internet is the place to be for some live, air traffic control action. Find out for yourself what it's like in an air traffic control tower at these Web sites:

- ☼ Listen to live air traffic control communications from around the world at http://www.liveatc.net.

- ☼ Go behind the scenes at the Dallas-Fort Worth Airport, one of the world's busiest airports at http://webevents.broadcast.com/simuflite.
- ☼ Eavesdrop on air traffic controllers at the John F. Kennedy Airport at http://jfktower.com/jfktwr.

ONLINE DESTINATIONS
- ☼ Discover the science of flight at http://www.ag.ohio-state.edu/flight.
- ☼ Take the great paper airplane challenge at http://teams.lacoe.edu/documentation/projects/math/airplane_sites.html.
- ☼ Learn about the Wright Brothers first attempts at flight at http://teams.lacoe.edu/documentation/projects/math/airplane_sites.html.
- ☼ Find out how airplanes fly at http://teams.lacoe.edu/documentation/projects/math/airplane_sites.html.
- ☼ Visit the Federal Aviation Agency (FAA) air traffic control command at http://www.fly.faa.gov/flyfaa/usmap.jsp.
- ☼ Take an online tour of the Museum of Flight at http://www.museumofflight.org.
- ☼ Try out Return to Flight games with NASA http://www.nasa.gov/audience/forkids/home/returntoflight.html

AT THE LIBRARY
READ ALL ABOUT IT
For a better understanding of how planes fly, why they fly, and how they navigate, read some of the following books.

Faber, Harold. *Airplane.* New York: Benchmark Books, 2005.
Graham, Ian. *Planes, Rockets and Other Flying Machines.* New York: Scholastic, 2000.

Lopez, Donald. *Flight: Discoveries Series.* New York: Barnes and Noble, 2003.

Oxlade, Chris. *Airplanes: Uncovering Technology.* New York: Firefly, 2006.

Platt, Richard. *Flight.* New York: Dorling Kindersley, 2006.

UP, UP, AND AWAY

Make your own paper airplanes with tips and ideas found in books such as:

Blackburn, Ken. *Kids' Paper Airplane Book.* New York: Workman, 1996.

Botermans, Jack and Jacob. *High-Flying Paper Airplanes.* New York: Sterling, 2005.

Robinson, Nick. *Super Simple Paper Airplanes.* New York: Sterling, 2005.

Schmidt, Norman. *Great Paper Fighter Planes.* New York: Sterling, 2005.

Stillings, Doug. *Klutz Book of Paper Airplanes.* Palo Alto, Calif.: Klutz, 2004.

While you're at it, make three different types of paper airplanes. Keep a log of which ones fly the farthest, highest, and straightest.

WITH THE EXPERTS

Federal Aviation Administration
800 Independence Avenue, SW
Washington, DC 20591-0004
http://www.faa.gov

National Air Traffic Controllers Association
1325 Massachusetts Avenue, NW
Washington, DC 20005-4171
http://www.natca.org

GET ACQUAINTED

Gregory Mueller,
Air Traffic Controller

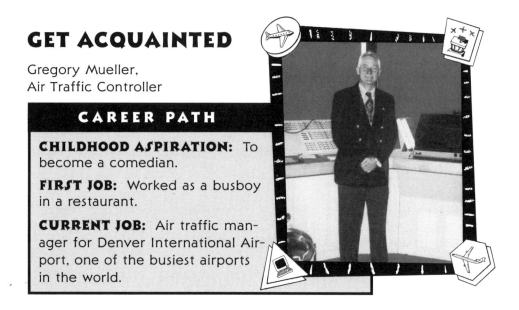

CAREER PATH

CHILDHOOD ASPIRATION: To become a comedian.

FIRST JOB: Worked as a busboy in a restaurant.

CURRENT JOB: Air traffic manager for Denver International Airport, one of the busiest airports in the world.

BEEN THERE, DONE THAT

Gregory Mueller has devoted more than 30 years to his work with the Federal Aviation Administration. During his career, he has worked in many different places as an air traffic controller or manager. He spent much of his time in the midwest, including six years at Chicago's O'Hare Airport. O'Hare is a busy intersection for airplanes, so he got lots of experience there! He also spent some time in California and then headed back to Denver.

Over the years he has watched technology change and improve the way controllers handle air traffic. He has frequently updated his skills by learning how to use new, state-of-the-art equipment and appreciates how it has made his job easier as well as making air travel safer for planes and people. On the horizon, he's looking forward to even better technology and the improvements it will bring.

NEVER A DULL MOMENT

One of the most challenging jobs he's ever had is his present one as the air traffic manager at Denver's airport. Three years before the airport even opened, he was on the job, planning and getting ready. He wanted to be sure that things went smoothly when planes began to take off and land at the new facility.

This meant testing procedures and equipment. It meant being there for airplanes that wanted to land to check the facility out. It meant hiring new people and getting them trained. It meant lots of coordination with local officials and administrators. Closing down the old airport, working with others to be sure that the new one opened on time, and making sure everything was operating correctly were major tasks.

Once the airport was up and running, Mueller was responsible for all the activities of the tower and for the safety of all the planes in the air around the airport and as they take off and land.

A GOOD CONTROLLER
Mueller says that one of the most important skills of a good controller is the ability to think fast—even with lots of distractions! He must be able to do many things at once. He must also be able to visualize the relationships of planes in the air just by looking at a little radar screen.

He's found that the only way to be ready to handle all this mentally is to be in top physical shape. Mueller works out regularly to keep at his best. A good workout also helps to relieve the stress that comes with the job.

WORLDWIDE CONNECTIONS
Controllers talk to one another as they pass the responsibility for an aircraft over to the next person. Each is a link in an intricate worldwide system of controllers and equipment. Mueller says it's fun to be part of that system and to know that you are "in touch" with others around the world who are doing the same thing.

Broadcaster

WHAT IS A BROADCASTER?

Broadcasters, also known as disk jockeys (DJs for short), radio announcers, newscasters, or just plain announcers, spend their time talking into a radio or television microphone. Depending on their designated roles, broadcasters might make announcements, read advertisements, or present the news. They scope out the weather and special events for listeners.

Whatever the forum, their job consists of three parts: to inform, entertain, and keep things on track. It can be quite a juggling act. The music or TV programs, the commercials, the news, and the broadcaster's comments have to be synchronized to fit within a very specific timeframe. It's the broadcaster's job to keep things running along without a hitch (such as embarrassing dead airtime or rambling dialogues). It takes total concentration to keep every second of airtime on track. It isn't easy,

NEWS WH34

but when someone tunes into their radio or television show, it has to sound and look as though it is.

Broadcasters working on live radio or television shows must be prepared to work crazy hours. A DJ hosting a morning show may have to be ready to hit the airwaves as early as 4 or 5 A.M. to reach the early rush-hour audience. Sometimes traffic reporters will work the morning rush hour and then come back for the evening rush hour. In addition, they prepare their reports, get information, do interviews, set up programs, and keep in touch with their listeners. It can make for a very long day.

Talk show hosts interview a wide variety of guests during either live or prerecorded segments. The show might be about a specific subject, about a guest's life, or about a timely topic. Talk show hosts rarely improvise when they do a show, even though the goal is often to sound as if they are engaged in a comfortable conversation with a good friend. They spend lots of time doing homework, learning as much as possible about the guest they will be talking with and the subject they will be discussing. Reading, researching, planning, and practice are regular features of the job.

Successful broadcasters of all varieties share some common traits, including

- a distinctive voice and great diction
- exceptional public speaking skills
- the ability to think on their feet
- strong people skills and empathy for others' concerns and opinions
- the curiosity to stay informed about current events

To become a broadcaster, a well-rounded education and a base of experience is generally required. Bachelor's degrees with a major in subjects such as journalism, English, communications, mass media, broadcasting, or liberal arts are good choices. Experience typically starts working behind the scenes at a radio or television station. It is not at all unusual for broadcasters to get their start in smaller towns and cities and work their way up to the major markets.

For someone with something to say, broadcasting can be an especially rewarding career choice.

☞ TRY IT OUT

HOST YOUR OWN SHOW
Take a tape recorder and do your own show. Arrange a time to interview one of your teachers (or maybe even your school principal). Before your scheduled meeting, learn as much as you can about the person and the issues you want to talk about (in other words, do your homework first). List your questions and stick to a reasonable time limit by keeping the conversation focused.

Once it's recorded, play it for your friends or your parents. Ask them to compare your interview to a radio show they often listen to.

VIEWS FROM THE STREET
With your trusty microphone and tape recorder handy, stand in the cafeteria during lunch hour. Ask a variety of students for their opinions about a hot issue currently being discussed at your school. For instance, ask what they think about a new rule, if they like the new lunch menu, or how they'd feel about going to school year-round. Another good opportunity for interviews is right after one of the sports teams has had a big win (or a big loss). Make sure to be prepared with questions before you start interviewing people.

TURN ON AND TUNE IN
For this activity, you'll need a computer and a television set. First, tune in to CNN, a major 24-hour news channel, at the beginning of any hour for the day's headline news. Listen carefully and take notes about major stories that they cover.

Next, go to CNN's Internet Web site (http://www.cnn.com). Read the reports about each of the major stories covered on television. Identify the main points in each article and check your notes to see which ones where covered on the telecast. Compare the similarities and differences between a live report and a written one.

✔ CHECK IT OUT

🖱 ON THE WEB
ADJUST YOUR INTERNET DIALS
Who needs a radio when you can go online to hear some of your favorite tunes? Some online radio stations to try include:

- Crazy Dave's Kid Show at http://www.crazydaveradio.com
- Kidzworld Radio at http://www.kidzworld.com/radio
- New York Kids at http://www.nykids.org
- Radio KOL http://aolsvc.kol.aol.com/radio_oc.adp
- Radio Disney at http://radio.disney.go.com

📚 AT THE LIBRARY

Find out more about what it's like to work in broadcasting in book such as:

Cupp, David. *Television Reporter.* Chanhassen, Minn.: Child's World, 2006.

McAlpine, Margaret. *Working in Film and Television.* Milwaukee, Wisc.: Gareth Stevens, 2004.

Somervill, Barbara. *Backstage at a Broadcast.* Danbury, Conn.: Children's Press, 2003.

And for those interested in sports broadcasting, relive some great moments in broadcasting in these books:

Garner, Joe. *And the Fans Roared: The Sports Broadcasts that Kept Us on the Edge of Our Seats.* Chicago: Sourcebooks, 2000.

———. *And the Crowd Goes Wild: Relive the Most Celebrated Sports Events Ever Broadcast.* Chicago: Sourcebooks, 2002.

🗣 WITH THE EXPERTS

American Federation of
Television and Radio Artists
260 Madison Avenue
New York, NY 10016-2401
http://www.aftra.org/aftra/aftra
.htm

Broadcast Education Association
1771 N Street NW
Washington, DC 20036-2891
http://www.beaweb.org

National Association of
Broadcasters
1771 N Street NW
Washington, DC 20036-2800
http://www.nab.org

Radio and Television News
Directors Association
1600 K Street NW, Suite 700
Washington, DC 20006-2838
http://www.rtnda.org

GET ACQUAINTED

Peter Jones, Radio Host

CAREER PATH

CHILDHOOD ASPIRATION: To be a forest ranger.

FIRST JOB: Polishing brass bed frames, brass candelabras, brass lamps, and other brass products at a brass shop.

CURRENT JOB: Storyteller, host, and producer of the syndicated children's radio program *Tell Us A Tale.*

TICKING THEIR FUNNY BONE

Peter Jones first learned he could hold the stage in the first grade, when he played an elf at a local elementary school in New Milford, Connecticut (where he grew up). The role called for a little acting, singing, and dancing. After he noticed the laughter from the audience, he decided to add a few extra ad-libbed lines and choreography of his own. The audience went wild, and he realized there was fun to be had performing.

By the time he was a teenager, Peter Jones wasn't sure what he wanted to do when he grew up, but he did know that whatever he did had to involve making people laugh. It was something he seemed to have a real talent for.

This natural talent surfaced again in college when he took an improvisation acting class. The talent followed him to Charlottesville, Virginia, where he moved after graduation and joined an improv acting troupe. There he began doing a lot of character studies and continued with improvisation in his spare time. He was preparing to move to New York City to continue it full time, when he met a storyteller and, you might say, found his destiny. The two joined forces—combining their improv and storytelling backgrounds.

A few months later, the duo was invited to be on a local children's radio show. Soon, they were offered their own radio show. Although, Jones and his first storytelling partner eventually went their separate ways, Jones kept at the radio show. After a couple of years of fiddling with the format, he developed *Tell Us A Tale* and soon thereafter began syndicating the program to radio stations around the United States (and online at http://www.TellUsATale.com).

A STORY IS BORN

Jones has a recording studio and office in his home, so he literally wakes up and goes right to work—after a walk with his dog, Shade, that is. These early-morning jaunts give him a chance to take in the wonders of nature and, with a little luck, get the creative juices flowing. Once he gets to the office, he goes over the stories he has recorded with his *Tell Us A Tale* colleague, Jen Hoffman, and comes up with different themes for each show. Once the stories and music are selected and timed (every second counts in radio broadcasting!), he writes and records voice-overs to introduce and "back announce" (what you say after a song or story has ended) each segment of the show. One all the segments are ready, he goes back and double-checks the time to make sure each show is precisely 28 minutes long. With just the right amount of material ready, he then sits down at his computer and begins mixing the segments (theme song, stories, tunes, and introductions/back announcing) together.

Once the show is complete, he sends it to the different stations that carry *Tell Us A Tale* in syndication. In the old days, he had to mail them out on CDs. But now he can send them through the Internet, which saves both time and money.

MORE THAN MEETS THE EAR

Like most jobs, Jones's has good and bad parts. The best part, he says, is creating something for others to enjoy. Before he goes to bed each night, he always asks himself if he has made at least one person happy that day. With the show airing on so many stations (and online), most days there is a pretty good chance that the answer to this question is yes!

Jones says that the worst part about the job is having to do the "office work" himself. He has to fill out paperwork, send the shows, handle promotions, book performances (for both live radio appearances and storytelling), and all the other details that come with running a regular broadcast. There is much more to the job than what the listener gets to hear.

Of course, he says his biggest job is to keep the listener from changing the channel. So he spends a lot of time trying to come up with fun ways to tie everything together. Oftentimes that means telling embarrassing stories about himself or friends and family members—but not without getting their permission first.

LISTEN UP, FUTURE RADIO HOSTS

Jones says that anyone who wants to do what he does needs to find ways to talk in front of others. Whether it is just telling jokes or performing in a play or musical, do it, he encourages. The more you talk, the better you get. The old joke asking how you can get to Carnegie Hall (Answer: Practice, practice, practice!) is true whatever you do in life. That and have fun doing it.

TAKE A TRIP!

Corporate Trainer

SHORTCUTS

SKILL SET

✔ BUSINESS
✔ TALKING
✔ WRITING

GO get involved in your school's debate team.

READ the business section of your local newspaper or the _Wall Street Journal_ classroom edition online at http://www.wsjclassroomedition.com.

TRY teaching one of your friends how to do something they have never done before.

WHAT IS A CORPORATE TRAINER?

Corporate trainers are to the business world what school teachers are to your world. They are the people who teach, train, inform, motivate, and educate businesspeople on topics ranging from business etiquette to the latest computer technology.

To succeed in this specialized area of adult education, a corporate trainer must be a team builder, a public speaker, and a good listener. He or she must be comfortable speaking in front of both large and small groups of businesspeople and must possess the presentation skills necessary to get and keep the attention of his or her audience.

Training business professionals is quite different from teaching children. The "students" come with much more experience and higher expectations, and quite often they have paid a significant amount of money to be there. The corporate trainer's job is to value their experience, meet their expectations, and give them their money's worth.

Corporate trainers generally must become experts in at least three areas, including

☼ Communication skills. Remember, successful communication involves both giving and receiving information. Corporate trainers must be skilled in giving public presentations and in receiving student feedback.

43

Corporate Trainer

🔆 Business skills. In order to train others, a corporate trainer has to know something that others want to learn. Whether it's marketing, technology, or personal development skills, the trainer has to know all there is to know about their topic.

🔆 Adult education skills. Knowing what techniques work best with a professional audience is key to a successful training session.

A good corporate trainer or public speaker can motivate his or her audience to feel better about themselves and their abilities. The trainer encourages the audience to think in a whole different way, to look at a problem from a new angle, or to test out fresh skills.

As is true for many careers, there are quite a few routes to becoming a corporate trainer. Some corporate trainers begin their careers as teachers, and some get their start working within the human resources system of a larger company, while others are very experienced professionals who have accumulated a lot of information to share with others. Corporate trainers can work as the employees of a corporation or may offer their services to any number of clients as private consultants.

Preparing to become a corporate trainer is varied. Because the profession often involves interfacing with a well-educated audience, a strong educational background is important. This can take the form of degrees in education, business, communication, or any number of specialized areas. Experience is also an important part of building credibility as a trainer.

In our world's ever-changing workplace, keeping up with the latest skills, technology, and information is necessary for survival in business. Corporate trainers play a big role in keeping the workforce ready and able to tackle new challenges.

 **TRY IT OUT**

BUILD A BETTER SANDWICH

Gather several friends together in your kitchen. Show them how to make your favorite sandwich. Be sure you take it step by step. Build it up and make it great! Find out if everyone else likes it as much as you do. If they don't, find out what they would do to improve it.

TEACHER FOR A DAY

Talk to one of your teachers. Volunteer to teach part of a class. Spend lots of time preparing. Be sure you know everything you can about the subject you will teach.

Put together a written lesson listing all the information you want to share and any specific facts you need to remember. Get some feedback and comments from your teacher about how you did. Talk to your classmates. What did they learn from your lesson? Or, if trying to teach your friends seems a little too scary for now, find out if your school has any programs where older students tutor younger ones.

THE TOAST OF THE TALK

Toastmasters International is an organization that consists of about 8,000 clubs all over the world. These clubs get together to help each other improve their public speaking skills. It's a great source of high-quality, low-cost communication training. While the main clubs are only available to people who are 18 and older, Toastmasters also provides great resources for youth leadership clubs.

If there isn't already a club up and running in your area, you'll have to find a local club or adult willing to sponsor a new club. Go online to http://www.toastmasters.org to find out what's available in your area.

✔ CHECK IT OUT

🖱 ON THE WEB

PEOPLE ARE STILL TALKING ABOUT IT

Go online to hear some great speeches that people are still talking about years—even decades—after they were first delivered. See what you can learn from some of these masters of communication:

- 💡 History Channel Speeches and Video at http://www .historychannel.com/broadband/home/
- 💡 The History Place Great Speeches Collection at http:// www.historyplace.com/speeches/previous.htm
- 💡 American Rhetoric Top 100 Speeches at http://www .americanrhetoric.com/top100speechesall.html

📚 AT THE LIBRARY

READ YOUR WAY TO SUCCESS

People will be more likely to listen to people who have their acts together. Start getting ready to make the most of your teen years with some of the tips found in books such as:

Brain, Marshall. *The Teenagers Guide to the Read World*. New York: Prentice Hall, 1997.

Carlson, Richard. *Don't Sweat the Small Things for Teens*. New York: Hyperion, 2000.

Covey, Sean. *7 Habits of Highly Effective Teens*. New York: Fireside, 1998.

Foster, Chad. *Teenagers Preparing for the Real World: Formulas for Success*. Lithonia, Ga.: Rising Books, 1999.

McGraw, Jay. *Life Strategies for Teens*. New York: Fireside, 2000.

🗣️ WITH THE EXPERTS

American Society for Training
and Development
1640 King Street
PO Box 1443
Alexandria, VA 22313-2043
http://www.astd.org/astd

National Association of
Workforce Development
Professionals
810 First Street, NE, Suite 525
Washington, DC 20002-4227
http://www.nawdp.org

National Speakers Association
1500 South Priest Drive
Tempe, AZ 85281-6203
http://www.nsaspeaker.org

Toastmasters International
PO Box 9052
Mission Viejo, CA 92690-9052
http://www.toastmaster.org

GET ACQUAINTED

Jerome Jewell, Corporate Trainer

CAREER PATH

CHILDHOOD ASPIRATION: To be an architect or jet pilot.

FIRST JOB: Mowing lawns one summer in Queens, New York.

CURRENT JOB: President of his own consulting company, Jewell Consulting Group.

GONE FISHING

"Give someone a fish, and you feed him for a day. Teach someone how to fish, and you feed him for a lifetime." As a corporate trainer, Jerome Jewell feels he is teaching employees how to fish.

Jewell worked his way up in a very large corporation. When he first was put in a leadership position, he found that giving employees some training helped them develop as individuals. This, in turn, made them better employees. As he got more involved in training people, he discovered he really liked it—and was good at it. He also discovered that the key to effective training was not telling someone what to do or how to act but helping them learn how to think about their jobs.

He now spends most of his time training employees for big companies. He helps them figure out how to be more productive and to work together with others for better results. He does this all over the world.

DIFFERENT CULTURES

Have you ever wondered what would happen if you got 10 people together and asked them to agree about how to do something? If each of those 10 people came from a different country, with a different cultural background, speaking a different language, it might be hard to get them to agree on anything.

Jewell works with this type of situation often. He finds it fascinating to watch the interaction between people when they are trying to figure out a problem. A person from Mexico will think differently about things than a person from Germany. They have different ideas because they have different experiences. If there isn't a common language between them, it will be harder for them to communicate. But Jewell makes it happen.

LIGHTBULBS

When his students find the solution to the problem, he says it's like turning a light on in a dark room. When this happens, he knows that the changes being made are long lasting. This is Jewell's favorite part of his job.

Often he will have a former student call him and say: "You really changed my life. Thank you. Here's what happened to me." He loves hearing their success stories.

He remembers having a woman come up to him after one class. She was in tears when she told him she had just been promoted to supervisor in a large organization. It seemed that everyone except her was convinced that she had what it would take to be successful. All her friends and coworkers urged her to "go for it!" She didn't think she could. Jewell asked the right questions and helped her to see for herself that she had the ability to make it.

LISTEN. DON'T TALK
A corporate trainer must be a good listener. Jewell says that a corporate trainer must like to listen almost more than he or she likes to talk. A good trainer will help students find their own solutions. This is achieved by asking questions and guiding people in their search, not by telling them right away what the answer is.

This takes a lot of self-discipline. It also helps to recognize that teachers and trainers learn from their students as much as their students learn from them.

IF AT FIRST YOU DON'T SUCCEED . . .
You may have to try out a lot of possibilities before you find the best approach. When Jewell had his first job cutting grass in the summer, he had lots of people telling him how to trim the lawn. Everyone had a different idea.

Some of those early trainers would demonstrate the "right way" for a few feet, and then he would have to finish the rest. Others would simply try to tell him the right way. He found out that in order to really learn it, he had to do it himself. A learning-while-earning approach is one that he heartily recommends.

HIS ADVICE TO YOU
Don't become a corporate trainer because you think you will make lots of money. Do it because you love to help people improve themselves. The money will follow. It can be draining emotionally, but if you go into it with your whole heart, it can be richly rewarding far beyond any money you will be paid.

Flight Attendant

SHORTCUTS

GO take a tour of the airport nearest you.

READ Flight Attendant by Rosemary Wallner (Minneapolis: Capstone, 2000).

TRY serving a meal in a nursing home nearby.

SKILL SET

✔ TALKING

✔ TRAVEL

✔ SCIENCE

WHAT IS A FLIGHT ATTENDANT?

Flight attendants have two priorities. The first, and most important, is to be sure the passengers and crew on board an aircraft are safe. The second is to make the flight as comfortable and pleasant an experience as possible. This is where the beverages, smiles, and onboard movies come in handy.

The main reason flight attendants are on board is to ensure that the safety regulations of the Federal Aviation Administration (FAA) are followed. If an emergency arises during a flight, flight attendants must be prepared to handle it. They must be ready to open emergency exits, be sure oxygen is available if needed, check to be sure seat belts are securely fastened, and help passengers get out quickly in a crisis. They also have to be ready to give first aid if someone gets sick while the plane is in the air.

When the flight attendants are not involved in seeing to the safety of the passengers, they are seeing to their comfort. This includes serving beverages and meals. This process involves pushing 200-pound beverage and meal carts up and down a very narrow aisle and using every people-pleasing skill they possess to keep a planeload of passengers satisfied.

Meals might be anything from a bag of peanuts and a beverage to a seven-course meal on an international flight in the first-class section. The flight attendant may have to prepare it, heat it up, or just unwrap it, depending on the type of food served.

Meals aren't the only service-oriented task that a flight attendant must take care of. There are the children flying without a supervising adult to keep an eye on. Passengers with special needs such as dietary restrictions and physical disabilities must be accommodated. Then, of course, there is the hard-to-please passenger who keeps things interesting. Keeping track of everyone's needs requires diplomacy, tact, and great communication skills.

Before takeoff, the flight attendants are briefed on special problems and possible weather conditions along the route that might make the flight bumpy or hazardous. They also must check to be sure that the safety equipment aboard the aircraft is in working order and ready at a moment's notice. In addition, they ensure that the cabin is clean and neat, meals and beverages are ready, and headsets and the public address system are working and that plenty of newspapers and magazines are on hand for the passengers to read.

Flight attendants work different schedules depending on the airline. They may work three to four days and have the rest of the week off. Their flying time each day is limited and they must have a specific amount of break time in between trips (among other rules), so they can be alert and ready to keep passengers safe. With so many flights going to so many different places in the world, scheduling can get pretty tricky.

Flight attendants must be prepared to go anywhere at a moment's notice. Can you imagine being ready to fly to Alaska, getting to the airport, and having the airline tell you that they really need you to fly to Florida instead? So much for the sweaters in your suitcase.

While flight attendants don't have to have a college degree, they have to meet specific requirements and get lots of training from the airline before they start flying. They do this in a simulated plane environment. It looks and acts just like the real thing but doesn't have real passengers. The practice "plane" is actually a tin tube at ground level, not 35,000 feet. Much of the training process covers the many different kinds of emergencies that could occur and what to do about them if they do. Learning a second language provides an extra edge for getting hired and for working the more prestigious international flights.

☞ TRY IT OUT

CONFLICT RESOLUTION

The next time you have friends over to visit, try this activity. Gather about 25 different household items (or just write the names of different items on index cards), such as a tent, a flashlight, a solar battery, a book, and so on—be creative. Tell them that they have just been chosen to take a group trip to the moon, and they may take 10 of these items with them. The tricky part is that everyone has to agree on which items go and which ones stay. Your role is to act as mediator. Use the best diplomatic skills you can muster to bring the group to an agreement.

TRAVEL THE WORLD

Take an imaginary trip. Pick a place that you would like to go to. Using your library as a "jumping off point," find out all that you can about that place. Visit a travel agency or two to find out if there are any brochures, posters, or other travel information about your chosen destination. Call around to different airlines and find out what the flight schedule and costs would be. Plan an entire itinerary. Compile all the information in a travel journal, and look forward to the day when you make this travel dream come true.

BROADEN YOUR HORIZONS

If there's someone at your school whose native language is not English, ask them to teach you about their language and culture. Try to spend a little time with them each day, learning new words, swapping foods at lunch, and discovering the many things you have in common. Keep track of your progress by using a small notebook to record everything you learn each day.

 # ✔ CHECK IT OUT

🖱 ON THE WEB
INTERNET ALTITUDE

You'll find a variety of useful resources on the Internet. Start at the Flight Attendants Resource Center. Here you'll find links to specific resources, information about minimum hiring requirements, and access to the Web sites for specific airlines. The Internet address is http://www.flightattendants.org.

Explore the world with a little help from these Web sites:

- 💡 Find out how far it is between any two cities in the world at http://www.indo.com/distance.
- 💡 Take off on a virtual global adventure at the National Geographic for Kids Web site at http://www.national geographic.com/kids.

☼ Check out a kid-friendly travel guide at http://www
.travelforkids.com.
☼ You'll wish you were here with postcards from all 50
states at http://www.postcardsfrom.com.
☼ Plan the GeoGame online at http://www.global
schoolnet.org/GSH/project/gg.
☼ All aboard the United Nation's Cyber School Bus at
http://www.un.org/Pubs/CyberSchoolBus.

📚 AT THE LIBRARY

AROUND THE WORLD READING

Until you are old enough to travel the world as a flight attendant, books provide the next best thing to being there. A
few of the many books you can read to discover more about
the fascinating people and places of the world include:

Croze, Harry. *Africa for Kids: Exploring a Vibrant Continent.*
Chicago: Chicago Review Press, 2006.
Editors of World Almanac. *World Alamanac for Kids.* New
York: World Almanac, 2006.
Goodard, Phillippe. *Kids Around the World: We Live in India.*
New York: Harry Abrams, 2006.
Gruber, Beth. *National Geographic Countries of the World:
Mexico.* Washington, D.C.: National Geographic, 2003.
Phillips, Dee. *People of the World.* Greenville, Wisc.: School
Speciality, 2006.
Pilon, Pascal. *Kids Around the World: We Live in China.* New
York: Harry Abrams, 2006.
Smith, David. *If the World Were a Village: A Book About the
World's People.* Tonawanda, New York: Kids Can, 2002.
Underwood, Deborah. *Where Are Your Manners?: Cultural
Diversity.* Chicago: Raintree, 2006.

🗣 WITH THE EXPERTS

Association of Flight Attendants
501 Third Street NW
Washington, DC 20001-2760
http://www.afanet.org

Future Aviation Professionals of America
4959 Massachusetts Boulevard
Atlanta, GA 30337-6607

GET ACQUAINTED

Lori Hurd, Flight Attendant

CAREER PATH

CHILDHOOD ASPIRATION: To be a mom and a flight attendant.

FIRST JOB: Baby-sitting.

CURRENT JOB: Flight attendant for national airline.

WISHES CAN COME TRUE

For as long as Lori Hurd can remember, she has wanted to do two things: be a mom and be a flight attendant. She's happy to report that both of her wishes came true. First came the mom part. She spent many years staying at home to raise her two daughters, Audra and Chelsea. Although she still wanted to be a flight attendant, she decided that children and constant travel weren't the right mix for her family. So while her girls where young she focused her energy on taking care of them.

All that changed once her eldest daughter went off to college and the other one got busy with high school. That's when a help-wanted ad in the newspaper caught Hurd's attention. It stated that one of her favorite airlines was looking for flight attendants and gave details about a meeting where people could go for more information. She, along with 600 other aspiring flight attendants, attended the meeting and found out that the company had just 45 positions available.

Needless to say, going from 600 applications to 45 positions involved a rigorous narrowing-down process. The process started with a group interview where Hurd and a couple dozen other people were asked a variety of questions and had to answer them in front of each other. The people who handled themselves with the most ease and confidence were invited back for further interviews. Hurd says that throughout the extensive interview process, the company tried to find people who were friendly and outgoing as well as professional and serious about safety. Most of all, they were looking for people who enjoy people and love to travel.

Several interviews later, Hurd was offered a chance to participate in the airline's six-week training program. There she learned about federal aviation regulations (important rules that flight attendants call FARs), how to conduct emergency evacuations on ground and in water, and how to deal with difficult passengers and handle irregular situations.

UP, UP, AND AWAY

Now, several years later, Hurd says she has been delighted to discover that working as a flight attendant is even better than she imagined. She typically works three or four days and then gets three or four days off. Although some flight attendants choose assignments where they fly out and return back to their home base every day, Hurd says that she prefers to pack her bags and stay in different cities while she's working. A typical run might include taking off from Denver, flying to Los Angeles, retuning to Denver, and flying out again for an overnight stay in Houston. Spending about seven hours in flight each day is average. Among Hurd's favorite destinations are Anchorage, San Diego, Seattle, and New York City.

Flying as much as she does, she's learned to spot subtle differences in the passengers. For instance, people tend to be friendlier on certain routes than others. She also says that flight attendants get to be with people during some of the best and worst times of their lives. Some are celebrating honeymoons or special vacations, while others are rushing to be with a sick loved one or are on their way to a funeral.

READY TO TAKE FLIGHT?

According to Hurd, answering a few quick questions can clue you in on whether or not a sky-high career is right for you:

- ☼ Do you enjoy travel?
- ☼ Do you like being around people for long periods of time?
- ☼ Are you curious about visiting new places?
- ☼ Do you get along well with all kinds of people?
- ☼ Are you flexible?

One of the first things Hurd found out about her job was that it wasn't like a typical nine-to-five office job. If someone gets on your nerves, there's no place to go chill out once the airplane takes off!

One of the best things she found out about being a flight attendant is that, for her, it's more like a gift than a job. She says some days she has to pinch herself to believe that she's getting paid to do something she loves so much.

Hotel Manager

SHORTCUTS

GO visit different kinds of hotels, inns, and restaurants in town.

READ all about the special things to see and do in your town.

TRY volunteering at your local chamber of commerce to give information to visitors about your community.

WHAT IS A HOTEL MANAGER?

Hotel managers have to oversee every detail at a hotel. They manage a large staff of people who divide up the many duties.

All the rooms must be cleaned every day. Added to that, the guests need to be greeted with a smile, checked into the hotel, and shown to their rooms. Luggage needs to be carried too. If your guests need to know about a good restaurant or special things to see in your town, you and your staff need to have the answers. Business conventions need space for meetings. Organizations need space to hold special events. Families need space to celebrate major occasions such as weddings. And, of course, all those guests will want to be entertained after their work is finished, so they'll be looking for the hotel's swimming pool, exercise room, and night clubs. Hotels, motels, and other hospitality establishments have to be prepared to handle these needs and more as "hosts" to any number of overnight guests.

Hotel accommodations run the gamut from the luxury, world-class hotel to the cozy bed-and-breakfast inn with the following types of accommodations in between:

- conference centers
- convention hotels
- executive suites
- health spas
- hotel and motel chains
- resorts
- roadside inns

Hotels can be big with room for lots of people to stay overnight, or they might be very small, with room for only a few people. If the manager actually lives at the hotel, he or she may have to be available 24 hours a day to serve the guests and take care of any situations that might occur. If it's a big hotel, that can mean lots of headaches!

The large hotels have people who specialize in taking care of different kinds of problems. Housekeeping will see that the beds are made and the rooms and bathrooms are clean. Maintenance workers will take care of plumbing, electrical, heating, and air-conditioning problems and see that equipment is up-to-date. Groundskeepers will be sure that the grass is cut, the flowers are at their best, and the walks are clean. The front desk will take reservations, check people into the hotel, be sure guests can pay for their rooms, and direct any complaints to the proper department.

In a typical larger hotel, managers handle specific functions of the operation in areas such as

assistant manager	general manager
convention service manager	housekeeping manager
food services manager	reservations manager
front service manager	resident manager

Small hotels are sometimes called motels, inns, or bed-and-breakfasts. With a very small inn, the owner may be handling all the different tasks by him- or herself.

At a bed-and-breakfast inn (B&B), people spend the night and have breakfast in the morning. In this type of hotel, very often the owner will cook breakfast, clean the rooms and the bathrooms, change the beds, check people in, take reservations, take care of repairs, tell people about special places to visit, and recommend restaurants. It's lots of work, but owners have the chance to meet many people and talk with them.

Dealing with lots of different people is part of every hotel manager's job. Sometimes these people are happy with the service you provide. Sometimes they are not. Strong communications skills, diplomacy, stamina, and lots of charm are valuable assets for hotel managers.

Training requirements for hotel/motel managers vary almost as much as the many types of places where people can spend the night. Some smaller hotels and chains require only high school graduation or an associate's degree in a hospitality-related field. Count on the major chains and more service-oriented places to require more education—a bachelor's in hospitality management for assistant managers and graduate work in hotel administration or business management for general managers. In addition, many hotel corporations offer in-house training opportunities to its management staff.

☞ TRY IT OUT

HAVE A B&B SLEEPOVER

If you have the room at your house, and if your parents say it's OK, host a B&B (bed & breakfast) sleepover. Prepare "rooms" (even if it's just a separate space with a sleeping bag). Add any special touches you can think of and your budget can afford—potpourri, cute little soaps, magazines, a water bottle, and other comforts are safe bets.

Invite a few friends and have them arrive just after dinner. Provide a snack (fresh, warm cookies are great, or maybe popcorn). Have a fun activity organized. Some suggestions: play a game (charades might be fun), watch a movie, do a puzzle, or whatever you think your guests would enjoy. Use your imagination for this part.

WELCOME TO MY HOME TOWN

Imagine that you are a hotel manager in the nicest hotel in your town. Your first job is to put together a sightseeing brochure describing the places people visiting your town will want to see. Keep it kid-friendly and include information about the places you most like to shop, eat, and play.

HOTEL KID

The owners of a new national chain of hotels have invited you, the kid expert, to help them design a hotel that's just for kids. Think about it. What features would a kid-pleasing hotel need to have? Use words or pictures to describe your dream hotel. What kinds of food should it serve? Activities? What would the rooms look like? Get creative and have fun!

In the morning, have hot chocolate ready for a "wake-up" drink. Fix your guests a nice breakfast. Help them gather up their possessions before they leave, and see them off with a smile. But remember, once the guests are gone, some of your work is just beginning. Be sure to change the sheets, clean the bathrooms, and return your house back to normal.

✔ CHECK IT OUT

🖱 ON THE WEB

CYBER HOTELS

Check out some of favorite national hotel chains online at Web sites such as:

- 💡 Best Western at http://www.bestwestern.com
- 💡 Econolodge at http://www.econolodge.com
- 💡 Hilton at http://www.hilton.com
- 💡 Holiday Inn at http://www.holidayinn.com
- 💡 Hyatt at http://www.hyatt.com
- 💡 Marriott at http://www.marriott.com
- 💡 Ritz Carlton at http://www.ritzcarlton.com

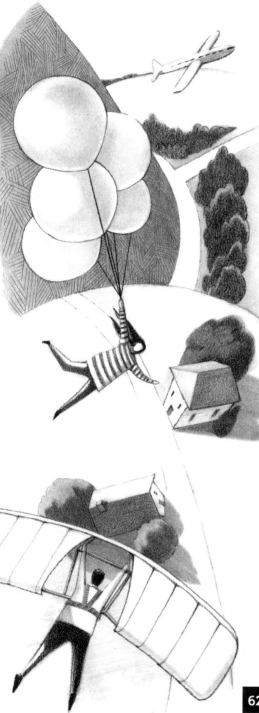

Based on what you discover online, which hotel would you most like to visit? Which one would you most like to work with?

📚 AT THE LIBRARY

FUN AND GAMES

Good hotel managers keep a few tricks up their sleeve for keeping guests entertained. Get some practice by throwing the world's best parties (slumber and otherwise) with tips found in books such as:

Brian, Sarah Jane. *Party Secrets: Who to Invite, Most Loved Munchies, Must Dance Music and Foolproof Fun.* Middleton, Wisc.: Pleasant Company, 2003.

Burly, Cylen. *Pajama Party Undercover.* New York: Grosset and Dunlap, 2003.

Griffin, Margaret. *Sleepover Book.* Tanawanda, New York: Kids Can, 2001.

Hunt, Sara. *Snooze-a-Palooza: More Than 100 Slumber Party Ideas.* Middleton, Wisc.: Pleasant Company, 2004.

Rhatigan, Joe and Rain Newcomb. *Run, Jump, Hide, Slide, Splash: The 200 Best Outdoor Games Ever.* Asheville, N.C.: 2005

🗣< WITH THE EXPERTS

International Council on Hotel, Restaurant and Institutional
  Education
2810 North Parham, Suite 230
Richmond, VA 23294-4422
http://chrie.org/

International Executive Housekeepers Association, Inc.
1001 Eastwind Drive, Suite 301
Westerville, OH 43081-3361
http://www.ieha.org

National Restaurant Association Educational Foundation
175 West Jackson Boulevard, Suite 1500
Chicago, IL 60604-2814
http://www.nraef.org

Professional Association of Innkeepers International
207 White Horse Pike
Haddon Heights, NJ 08035-1703
http://www.paii.org

GET ACQUAINTED

Rose Forbes, Innkeeper

CAREER PATH

CHILDHOOD ASPIRATION: To be a singer or dancer.

FIRST JOB: Working at Burger King.

CURRENT JOB: Innkeeper at Green Mountain Bed and Breakfast in Candler, North Carolina.

A FAMILY AFFAIR

After years of traveling across the country and international-
ally with their jobs, Rose Forbes and her husband Jack started

looking for a way to stay home and enjoy their family life. Having experienced the best and worst of hotel accommodations during their business travels, they agreed that they liked staying in bed-and-breakfasts best. It was more personal and allowed them to learn more about the places they were staying. So the idea of opening a bed-and-breakfast appealed to them. It could provide a good way to let them earn a living from home. Plus, it was an opportunity to create a unique lifestyle in a place they really wanted to live.

But first they had to figure out where that place was. Forbes says they spent four months looking at different places all over the country to set up their B&B. They looked in Colorado but decided the weather was a bit too cold. They looked in Texas but determined that the weather was a bit too hot for their liking. Finally, they settled on a community in the mountains of western North Carolina. There, a little like Goldilocks, they found that the weather was just right.

They also found an ideal property that a doctor had used as a combination home and office that had just enough space for their family home on one side and guest rooms and a dining room on the other. They set about renovating the property, decorating it, and learning all they could about how to be innkeepers.

The result, Green Mountain Bed and Breakfast, offers four comfortable guest suites in a beautiful natural setting. A pool, therapeutic hot tub, and lovely gardens complete the tranquil environment they created for their guests.

GOING GREEN

Forbes wanted to do more than provide a place where guests could eat and sleep, so she's gone to great lengths to create a unique, "green" atmosphere in both her bed-and-breakfast and her home. "Green" means that everything in the facility is chemical and toxin free. Food, cleaning products, furniture, and even the building materials are as natural as possible. Going green took lots of extra effort to research and cultivate, but Forbes says that it offers her guests a healthy getaway that is especially good for people with environmental allergies and food intolerances and who are health conscious.

Forbes's background in marketing, sales, and customer service all come into play as she runs the day-to-day aspects of the business and gets the word out to prospective guests. She hopes eventually to expand the facility to include seven guest rooms (the property includes a 12-car garage that can be converted into housing) and perhaps even an event center where people can enjoy the beautiful, natural setting for weddings and other special occasions.

WHAT'S FOR BREAKFAST?

While the 40-some Victorian-style bed-and-breakfasts nearby serve traditional breakfasts of eggs and bacon, Forbes decided to distinguish her meals by serving healthy, organic, gourmet breakfasts. A certified nutritional consultant, Forbes uses her expertise to plan and prepare meals that are good and good for you. She admits that some people think the meals are a bit weird or offbeat at first. But most are surprised at how tasty and filling they are. A typical breakfast might include a chilled melon soup and breakfast salad. Soup and salad for breakfast? Forbes encourages you to try it and shares her recipe for Green Mountain Organic Breakfast Salad to get you started:

    2 cups spring mix lettuce
    16 grape tomatoes cut in half
    16 mandarin orange sections
    1 cup Yukon gold potatoes cut in cubes
    1 package smoked tempeh strips, diced
    4 hard boiled eggs, diced
    Coconut oil
    Dressing:
    4 tablespoons extra virgin olive oil
    1 cup orange juice
    1 cup maple syrup

Cook potatoes and tempeh strips separately in coconut oil. Allow to cool. Assemble salad with lettuce on bottom, and add tomatoes, mandarin oranges, potatoes, eggs, and then tempeh strips on top. Add dressing and serve.

Law Enforcement Officer

SHORTCUTS

SKILL SET

✓ ADVENTURE

✓ SPORTS

✓ TALKING

GO ride with a police officer on patrol. Call your local police department to ask if they have a ride-along program.

READ any Nancy Drew mystery by Carolyn Keene or Hardy Boys mystery by Franklin Dixon.

TRY volunteering as a crossing guard or hall monitor for your school.

WHAT IS A LAW ENFORCEMENT OFFICER?

There are lots of shows on television about police officers and detectives. You've probably watched some and may think you have a pretty good idea about what a law enforcement officer does. But it isn't all action adventure. You sure don't catch the bad guys in a nice, tidy hour; sometimes you never get them.

Law enforcement officers include police officers, detectives, and sheriffs. The field might also include special agents working for the Federal Bureau of Investigation, the Drug Enforcement Administration, the Border Patrol, or the U.S. Marshals Service. All of these people are responsible for enforcing different kinds of laws and have different kinds of responsibilities.

In a typical day, a police officer in a smaller community might be called upon to do lots of different things such as direct traffic, patrol a beat, calm a family fight, make an arrest, pick up a barking dog, or collect evidence to be used in court. He or she might also be asked to testify in court about an arrest or talk to young people in a school or elderly people in a nursing home. Police officers deal with people from many different walks of life—some very rich and some very poor, some educated and some illiterate. They wear lots of hats and do lots of jobs.

In a larger city, a police officer might specialize in a particular area such as chemical analysis, fingerprint identification, polygraph operation, or handwriting analysis. On the beat, he or she might ride a horse, a bicycle, or a motorcycle as a "mounted patrol." He or she might have a dog to work with as part of the canine corps and spend time looking for drugs or tracking kidnap victims. Some cities have special emergency response teams that are assigned to deal with certain types of problems, such as terrorism, snipers, burglary, vice, or drugs.

A special agent working for the government might guard the president of the United States or investigate a bombing or the illegal production or sale of alcohol or firearms. Other possible tasks could include enforcing the laws that prevent smugglers from bringing illegal items into this country, or tracking down some counterfeit money. Some special agents investigate people who cheat on their taxes, while others search for bank robbers and members of organized crime. Others specialize in background checks, determining if a person is trustworthy enough to work in a top security job.

To become a law enforcement officer, you must be at least 20 years old, be a U.S. citizen, and have a valid driver's license. You must pass certain written tests as well as some

basic physical ones for vision, hearing, and drug use. After passing those entrance hurdles, you must meet some fairly rigorous physical standards of endurance, strength, and agility. Needless to say, you have to clean record—free from any trouble and criminal activity—to even be considered as a law enforcement officer.

Most local police departments require at least a high school education. If you want to work as a special agent for the federal government, you may need a college degree in any number of subject areas. Find out what the specific requirements are for the specific type of law enforcement you hope to pursue.

☞ TRY IT OUT

WHO DUNNIT?

To complete this activity, you'll need a notebook and pen, plus access to either a computer to log in to Mystery Net for Kids at http://kids.mysterynet.com or a copy of a good five-minute mystery book such as:

Obrist, Jurg. *Complex Cases: Three Major Mysteries for You to Solve.* Minneapolis: Millbrook, 2006.
Smith, Steve. *Five Minute Mysteries.* New York: Sterling, 2003.
Walton, Rick. *Mini-Mysteries: 20 Tricky Tales to Untangle.* Middleton, Wisc: Pleasant Company, 2004.
———. *Mini-Mysteries: 20 More Tricky Tales to Untangle.* Middleton, Wisc.: Pleasant Company, 2004.
Weber, Ken. *Five Minute Mysteries.* Philadelphia, Pa.: Running Press, 2005.
———. *More Five Minute Mysteries.* Philadelphia, Pa.: Running Press, 2006.

Label one page in your notebook with the title of a specific mystery. Draw a line down the middle of the page. On one side, describe what you think happened or "who dunnit." On the other side, write the actual solution. How often do you get it right?

TRAFFIC COP

Make an appointment to talk with an officer at your local police station. Ask what kinds of things get drivers into trouble most often. Is it speeding? Parking? Failure to yield?

As you ride in the car with your parents, see if you observe any of these violations. Keep a notebook handy and record license plate numbers, location, time, and car type. At the end of a month, add up your numbers to find out how many tickets you could have issued if you'd been in uniform.

# CHECK IT OUT

🖱 ON THE WEB

LAW ENFORCEMENT WANNABES

Do you want to work in law enforcement some day? Get acquainted with some of your potential employers at Web site such as:

- ☼ Bureau of Alcohol, Tobacco, Firearms and Explosives at http://www.atf.gov/kids/index.htm
- ☼ Central Intelligence Agency at http://www.fbi.gov/fbikids.htm
- ☼ Federal Bureau of Investigation http://www.fbi.gov/fbikids.htm
- ☼ National Security Agency at http://www.fbi.gov/fbikids.htm
- ☼ United States Marshals at http://www.usmarshals.gov/usmsforkids/index.html

ONLINE INVESTIGATIONS

Go online to hone your investigative skills with these interesting (and fun) Web sites:

- ☼ Join the history detectives club at http://pbskids.org/historydetectives.
- ☼ Help track down the source of deadly infectious diseases at http://medmyst.rice.edu.

- The perfect spot for armchair detectives can be found at http://www.courttv.com/game/allgames.html.
- See if you can help find the culprit at http://pbskids .org/dragonflytv/show/forensics.html.
- Germs beware! The food detectives are here at http://www.fooddetectives.com.

AT THE LIBRARY

CURL UP WITH A GOOD MYSTERY

There's nothing like a good mystery to test your powers of deduction. Here are a few suggestions (ask your teacher or librarian for others):

Balliett, Blue. *Chasing Vermeer.* New York: Scholastic, 2006.

Doyle, Arthur Conan. *The Hound of the Baskervilles.* New York: Simon and Schuster, 2000. (And other titles in the classic Sherlock Holmes Mystery series)

Koninburg, E.L. *From the Mixed Up Files of Mrs. Basil E. Frankweiler.* New York: Simon and Schuster, 2002.

Rose, Malcom. *Frances Luke Harding, Forensic Investigator: Double Check.* New York: Houghton Mifflin, 2006. (And other titles in the Traces series)

Zindel, Paul. *The Phantom of 86th Street.* New York: Hyperion, 2002. (And other titles in the P.C. Hawke mystery series)

While you are reading, keep track of all the clues and your own suspicions in a notebook. Before you read the concluding chapter, piece together all the clues and write down the name of the person you most suspect. Finish reading and see if you were right.

WITH THE EXPERTS

Academy of Criminal Justice Sciences
PO Box 960
Greenbelt, MD 20768-0960
http://www.acjs.org

American Society of Criminology
1314 Kinnear Road
Columbus, OH 43212-1156
http://www.asc41.com

International Association of Chief of Police
515 North Washington Street
Alexandria, VA 22314
http://www.theiacp.org

National Council on Crime and Delinquency
1970 Broadway, Suite 500
Oakland, CA 94612
http://www.nccd-crc.org

National Sheriff's Association
1450 Duke Street
Alexandria, VA 22314-3490
http://www.sheriffs.org

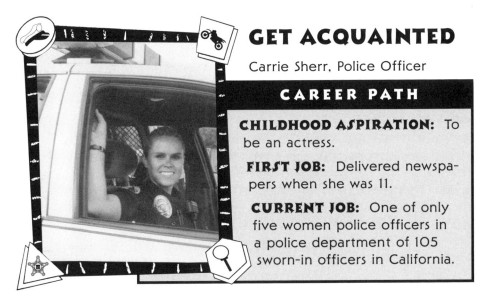

GET ACQUAINTED

Carrie Sherr, Police Officer

CAREER PATH

CHILDHOOD ASPIRATION: To be an actress.

FIRST JOB: Delivered newspapers when she was 11.

CURRENT JOB: One of only five women police officers in a police department of 105 sworn-in officers in California.

A DREAM FULFILLED

Carrie Sherr wanted to be an actress; in fact, that's what she focused on in college. It wasn't until she married a deputy sheriff that she realized that law enforcement was what she really wanted to do. She remembered a female D.A.R.E. (Drug Abuse Resistance Education) officer who spoke at her school when she was in the ninth grade. Sherr was impressed with her and with the possibilities for women in law enforcement.

MAKING A DIFFERENCE

For Sherr, the opportunity to make a difference in people's lives is what her job is all about. She remembers arresting two teenage girls for shoplifting. One girl had a prior arrest record. This girl, who wasn't the least bit sorry about what they had done, told Sherr that her friend had done all the stealing.

When Sherr talked with her friend, the second girl broke down into tears. Sherr spent some time talking to her, reminding her that she didn't have to live her life that way and that she could start right then to make a change. Evidently, that arrest and the talk with Sherr changed her life for the better. The second girl eventually wrote a thank-you letter to Sherr's police department.

Sherr says that working with kids, keeping them out of prison and off drugs, is her priority. She really wants to make a difference with young people.

MIRROR IMAGE

Sometimes being a police officer is similar to being a mirror. If Sherr stops someone and the person is belligerent and unkind, expecting that she will be too, she often finds it necessary to be extra firm. If someone treats her with respect and kindness, she mirrors that, making the "run-in with the law" a more positive experience.

A big part of being a police officer is keeping your cool when everyone else is losing theirs. An even temperament is a definite requirement. It's too easy to mirror the person you're talking to, and that isn't always good.

JUST FOR FUN

Sherr works out twice a day. Since physical fitness is such an important part of her job, she keeps herself in top shape. On any given day she may play racquetball in the morning and then work out in the gym in the evening. It's great for getting rid of the stress that piles up from the job.

ALL IN A DAY'S WORK

For Sherr, her fellow officers are like family. On a typical day she might work more than 12 hours, much of it with the same people.

Part of that time is spent patrolling—just being visible in the neighborhood. Most of her time (more than 70 percent) is spent on "activities": making arrests, pulling people over for traffic violations, stopping family disturbances. Keeping the peace (in other words, telling people to turn down the stereos and control the partying) is another big part of her job.

PAPERWORK GALORE

Sherr's job involves lots of paperwork. Laptops in the patrol cars have helped, but she still spends a lot of her time filling out forms and making reports. Good communication skills are a must. Law enforcement officers not only have to use verbal skills to help solve problems, but they also have to use their writing skills to submit a report about each incident.

SOME GOOD ADVICE

If you want to be a police officer, get involved in sports or other after-school activities. Keep busy. Stay out of trouble and away from drugs and alcohol. Live by the rules, since you'll have to enforce them later.

Minister/Priest/Rabbi

WHAT IS A MINISTER/PRIEST/RABBI?

Clergy are people who tend to the spiritual needs of others. Depending on the religion, clergy are called ministers, priests, rabbis, pastors, or preachers. These people lead religious services; organize worship and places of worship; visit elderly and sick people; and conduct funeral services, weddings, and other special services.

Some of them read from their religion's sacred texts, while others write sermons and then deliver them. At times they may also have to raise money to pay for special projects such as a new building or school, or to help a congregation member who needs assistance.

A big part of the job is counseling people. A clergy member might help a young couple get ready for marriage or work through a divorce. He or she might help someone who is sick or terminally ill. The clergy comfort families when someone dies. Often they just help someone see things in a more spiritual way.

Clergy must have a deep commitment to their own faith and their own spirituality. They must be rock solid in their own belief about who God is and who they are, and they must have a firm desire to build and maintain important relationships with others. In some religions, this might mean that they don't have a traditional family with a spouse and children.

Deeper values and spiritual thinking are absolutely necessary to becoming a member of the clergy. College and special religious training are required for many religions. Check out your place of worship to see what is required.

Sometimes the work of the clergy will extend beyond their own place of worship. Communities of different religions might get together to solve a common problem in the neighborhood. Often a clergy member will travel to other areas around the country to speak at different conferences. This interaction provides a way to discuss issues and beliefs with others, widening the clergy's perspective and influence.

Being a member of the clergy isn't a nine-to-five job. It's often more like a round-the-clock commitment. Emergencies and other human needs simply do not confine themselves to regular business hours. Choosing to become part of the clergy is essentially choosing a way of life.

Practicing what you preach is probably one of the most important and most difficult demands of the job. A big part of the job is to lead a congregation in embracing and living by the moral standards and spiritual values that the religion observes.

Deciding to join the clergy is an intensely personal choice. It's a profession that offers the opportunity to do more good for others than almost any other profession there is. It's not for everyone, but for those who feel drawn to serve in this way, it can be a richly rewarding decision.

👉 TRY IT OUT

TAG ALONG

If you are thinking about becoming a clergy member, learn as much as you can about the profession. Spend time with your own religious leader, as well as with others. Talk with them about their experiences and the demands of the profession. Ask if you can tag along as they perform some of their routine clerical duties—visiting the sick, preparing sermons, and planning worship services. Ask them for advice and counsel as you ponder this important decision.

WRITE A SERMON

Pick a subject or a favorite text from your religion's holy text that has special meaning for young people your age. Use a concordance and other references to find out all you can about what it means. Add your own thoughts to how it can be applied to everyday life.

Organize your discoveries into a sermon format. Show it to someone in the clergy and get his or her feedback on it. Ask if there might be an appropriate time to present your message to the youth group at your place of worship.

REACH OUT AND TOUCH SOMEONE

Ministering to others means more than just preaching to them. It involves a genuine investment in the lives of others. Find ways to make a difference in the lives of people in your community. Here are a few ideas.

- 💡 Visit a shut-in. This is someone who can't leave the house because of illness or old age. Help fix a meal, clean the house up a bit, or just chat for a while. Did you make him or her feel better just by being there?
- 💡 Get involved. Organize a canned food drive with the kids in your school. Take the cans you collect to a homeless shelter or a battered women's shelter.
- 💡 Show you care. Volunteer to play games with children staying in a foster home or orphanage.

✔ CHECK IT OUT

🖱 ON THE WEB
CYBER CHURCH
To find resources about a specific type of religion, use your favorite Internet search engine (http://www.google.com or http://www.yahooligans.com) to look for information. For instance, to find out about the Hindu faith type *Hindu*, type *Christianity* for Christianity, and so on. Other religions you might want to explore include Judaism, Buddhism, and Islam.

While you're at it, you might want to put together a chart to record your discoveries about things like deities, important beliefs, and, religions holidays. See what you can find out about the common values that all religions share—things like honesty, compassion, and justice.

📚 AT THE LIBRARY
BELIEVE IT OR NOT
People around the world express their faith in many different ways. Find out more about the world's religions in books such as:

Brown, Stephen. *World Religions: Protestantism*. New York: Facts On File, 2001.

Brown, Stephen, and Khaled Anatolios. *World Religions: Catholicism and Orthodox Christianity*. New York: Facts On File, 2006.

Hartz, Paula R. *World Religions: Baha'i*. New York: Facts On File, 2002.

———. *World Religions: Native American Religions*. New York: Facts On File, 2002.

———. *World Religions: Taoism*. New York: Facts On File, 2002.

Matthew, Gordon. *World Religions: Islam*. New York: Facts On File, 2001.

Morrison, Martha A. *World Religions: Judaism*. New York: Facts On File, 2002.

Nikky-Guninder, Kaur Singh. *World Religions: Sikhism*. New York: Facts On File, 2004.

Wandu, Madhu Bazaz. *World Religions: Buddhism*. New York: Facts On File, 2006.

———. *World Religions: Hinduism*. New York: Facts On File, 2006.

WITH THE EXPERTS

American Youth Work Center
1200 17th Street NW, 4th Floor
Washington, DC 20036-3006
http://www.youthtoday.org
http://www.friendsofvista.org

National Council of Churches
475 Riverside Drive
Suite 880
New York, NY 10115-0002
http://www.nccusa.org

National Interfaith Council
10190 North 106 Street
Scottsdale, AZ 85258-6025
http://www.nationalinterfaithcouncil.com

GET ACQUAINTED

Robert Gelinas,
Minister

CAREER PATH

CHILDHOOD ASPIRATION: To be an orthopedic surgeon.

FIRST JOB: Mowing lawns as a boy.

CURRENT JOB: Lead pastor, Colorado Community Church.

A LUCKY BREAK

When Robert Gelinas was in junior high, one of his favorite things to do was run. So when he broke his foot, not once, but twice over the course of a year, he didn't feel so lucky. The first time wasn't so bad. During the first surgery and medical treatment, he beame intrigued with the idea of becoming a doctor. He even started studying Latin to help prepare himself for a medical career.

When he broke the same foot just two months after the first cast came off, however, he really got discouraged. Lying in bed unable to do the one thing he loved most—run—he found himself in dire need of some comfort. Fortunately for him, he was at his grandmother's house. His grandmother always kept a Bible handy just for times like this. Thumbing through it, he came upon a passage in Proverbs (16:3) that says "Commit what you do to the Lord and you will succeed." He believes that it was at that precise moment that he felt God's call to become a minister.

JUST ONE SMALL PROBLEM

Having spent a lot of time at his neighborhood church with his grandmother, the idea of becoming a minister was not unwelcome; however, the more he thought about what ministers do, the more worried he became. That's because one of the most important things that ministers do is preach sermons and the thought of speaking in front of a crowd of people was pretty scary to Gelinas.

But once he started telling people whose opinions he valued about his desire to become a minister, they all confirmed that it was a good idea. Gelinas took this as a sign that he was on the right track and decided to trust God to take care of his public-speaking phobia. Apparently, his plan worked because although Gelinas confesses that he still gets butterflies in his stomach every time he starts to preach, this fear hasn't stopped him from becoming a very effective public speaker. He says that he's decided that his job is to faithfully explain the Scriptures in a loving way and that God is responsible for the rest.

EVEN MINISTERS HAVE BAD DAYS

Gelinas says that he considers a good day in the ministry to be one in which he has plenty of time to study and prepare his sermons (he spends at least 15 to 20 hours a week doing this). A good day isn't complete without additional time spent encouraging others in their faith and helping them learn how to be a positive influence in the world. Top this off with a little time to dream about the future of his church, and he'd call it a good day.

On the other hand, a bad day is spent smoothing ruffled feathers. Within his congregation, as with any close community, it's impossible not to hurt someome's feelings now and then. Start the day with a people crisis and end it with a batch of paperwork needing immediate attention, and you'll have just the right ingredients for the kind of day that Gelinas dreads.

PRACTICING WHAT HE PREACHES

As lead pastor of Colorado Community church, a multicultural, multicampus, interdenominational, and intergenerational church of over 3,500 people, Gelinas gets plenty of opportunity to preach. But much of his ministry's focus is on practicing what he preaches in meaningful ways. Not only is Gelinas the founder and president of a ministry called Project 1.27 that is devoted to helping children in Colorado's foster system find loving, permanent homes, but he is also the father of six children (five of whom were adopted). Not only does he pray for the poor, but his church actively pursues ministries like Lifeboat #14 to find ways to help them in practical and life-changing ways. You can find out more about Gelinas work at his church Web site at http://www.colorado community.org.

GO WITH WHAT YOU'VE GOT

Gelinas says that it didn't take long for him to discover what his strengths were as a minister. Teaching and leading are his strong points, so he finds ways to emphasize them in his work. He says that one of the most important things he's learned as a minister is to do what he does well and to give the others in his church a chance to do what they do well. It's a formula that has worked well with his various ministries.

According to Gelinas, it is also good advice for a young person trying to decide what to do with his or her life. Figure out what you do well and go with it!

News Reporter

SHORTCUTS

SKILL SET

✔ COMPUTERS

✔ TALKING

✔ WRITING

GO listen to the news on your local radio or television station.

READ your local newspaper every day.

TRY reporting the news yourself for your school's radio station or newspaper.

WHAT IS A NEWS REPORTER?

A news reporter works right in the middle of history in the making. Whether it's covering a tornado on the other side of town or a war on the other side of the ocean, reporters stay in the thick of the world's events.

A reporter strives to bring complete, unbiased accounts to his or her audience. A reporter on the trail of a newsworthy story (a "scoop," in industry terms) would find factual details as well as interesting features about the story from a variety of sources. Increasingly, reporters log on the Internet for up-to-the-minute news from around the world. The Internet also provides quick access to an incredible array of research materials. In addition, reporters might use other technological means of securing information quickly by making use of e-mail, a fax machine, or the ever-faithful telephone. They are also privy to news coming in over international wire services.

It is not at all unusual for a story to take reporters out of the office to the very place where the news is taking place. Once there, they get new information by interviewing witnesses or other people associated with the event. They may also be on hand to witness an event and provide eyewitness commentary on a story.

Reporters working for larger newspapers or television stations tend to specialize in a particular area of news such as sports, business, health, religion, politics, schools, crime, or consumer issues. These specialties are often referred to as "beats." Reporters working for a smaller paper or station may be required to cover more than one beat.

Within the broadcast journalism field (strictly TV or radio), specific jobs include:

anchor, who actually delivers the news on radio or television

investigative reporter, who tracks down the stories behind the headlines

correspondent, who reports from both foreign countries and major U.S. cities such as Washington, D.C.

general assignment reporter, who covers all kinds of stories, whenever and wherever they occur

Most reporters have a college degree specializing in journalism or communications. You can start preparing for a career in journalism now by taking courses in English, journalism, and social studies.

Experience is key to getting your foot in the door at any paper or station—large or small. Most large papers or stations want to see evidence of success at a smaller paper or station, and most smaller papers or stations want to see evidence of journalistic involvement in high school and college. So, experience with the yearbook, school newspaper, or community newspaper is a good start.

☞ TRY IT OUT

MAKE A TAPE
Check your community's paper for the important news. Pick the top stories and work them into a five-minute newscast. Tape it and play it back for your family or friends. If you have access to a video recorder, ask a friend to videotape your newscast.

LIVE FROM THE FAMILY TREE
Think of three people representing three different generations in your family—a kid, a parent, and a grandparent, for instance. Ask if you can practice your interviewing skills by asking them a few questions. Use a tape recorder or camcorder to record your sessions. See what you can find out about how their lives are different from yours. Are there any surprising similarities?

TAKE A TOUR
Call your local television news stations and ask if you can arrange for a tour of the facilities. Tell them that you are considering a career in journalism and want to see what it's really like to work at a TV station. With a little luck, you'll get the chance to see the equipment, the sound stage, and even an actual live newscast. With a little more luck, you may get the chance to talk with the reporters.

For a newsworthy virtual tour, go online to the Newseum at http://www.newseum.org.

✔ CHECK IT OUT

🖱 ON THE WEB
NETNEWS
Nothing beats the news coverage on the Internet. It's quick, it's thorough, and you have to read only what you want to know about. Go online and visit the Web sites of the following news stations:

💡 http://www.abcnews.go.com

- ☼ http://www.cbsnews.com
- ☼ http://www.cnn.com
- ☼ http://www.foxnews.com
- ☼ http://www.msnbc.msn.com
- ☼ National Geographic world news for kids at at http://news.nationalgeographic.com/kids
- ☼ Scholastic Kids's News at http://teacher.scholastic. com/scholasticnews/games_quizzes/index.asp

While you are there, pick one major story from the day's headline news. Compare the way each of these stations covers the story. Look for significant details that are included in one paper but not in another. Jot down the three main points of each story and pick out the various angles that each story emphasizes.

AT THE LIBRARY

A NOSE FOR NEWS

Find yourself hot on the trail of some newsworthy adventures in these books featuring young, fictional news reporters:

Christensen, Bonnie. *The Daring Nellie Bly: America's Star Reporter.* New York: Alfred Knopf, 2003.

Ellerbee, Linda. *Get Real 1: Girl Reporter Blows Lid Off Town.* New York: Harper Collins, 2000.

Feinsten, John. *Last Shot: A Final Four Mystery.* New York: Random House, 2006.

Trembath, Don. *The Popsicle Journal.* Custer, Wash.: Orca Books, 2002.

To find out what it's really like to be a journalist, don't miss:

Reeves, Diane Lindsey. *Virtual Apprentice: TV Jouranlist.* New York: Facts On File, 2007.

🗣️ WITH THE EXPERTS

Association for Education
  in Journalism and Mass
  Communication
234 Outlet Pointe Boulevard
Columbia, SC 29210-5667
http://www.aejmc.org

Dow Jones Newspapers Fund
PO Box 300
Princeton, NJ 08543-0300
http://djnewspaperfund.
  dowjones.com/fund

National Newspaper
  Association
PO Box 7540
Columbia, MO 65205-7540
http://www.nna.org

Newspaper Association of
  America Foundation
1921 Gallows Road, Suite 600
Vienna, VA 22182-3900
http://www.naa.org

Radio and Television News
  Directors Association and
  Foundation
1600 K Street NW, Suite 700
Washington, DC 20006-2838
http://www.rtnda.org

Society of Broadcast Engineers, Inc.
9102 North Meridian Street,
  Suite 150
Indianapolis, IN 46260-1896
http://www.sbe.org

GET ACQUAINTED

Mark Miller, News Reporter

CAREER PATH

CHILDHOOD ASPIRATION: To be an attorney or clergyman.

FIRST JOB: As a teenager, he peeled 200 pounds of onions a night in a sandwich shop.

CURRENT JOB: News director for WBAL in Baltimore, Maryland.

TOTALLY RESPONSIBLE

Although he started with the station as a news reporter, Mark Miller is now responsible for the entire news staff of the radio station. That means he oversees the reporting of the daily news of the nation, the city, and the world; it also includes weather, traffic, business, politics, and special events. He manages an annual budget of over $1 million!

Each day he holds "story meetings." He and his staff discuss what's going on that day, assign new stories, and map out the broadcast as best they can. Each reporter does what it takes to get the story together, writes it up, coordinates details such as special pre-taped interviews, and assumes responsibility for getting the story ready for broadcast.

THE EDWARD R. MURROW AWARD
In the broadcasting industry the most prestigious news award is the Edward R. Murrow Award. It's like getting an Oscar. Miller's station won six in the last four years for overall excellence in reporting and specifically for sports and feature reporting.

A few years ago the station won the award for an investigative report they did about the city comptroller. They did their homework and snooped around a bit, and they found out that money was being paid out to places it shouldn't have been. They uncovered the story and put an end to the waste and wrongdoing.

AN ENDURANCE TEST
Miller says one of the most important qualities of being a news reporter is having endurance. In 1987, in order to cover a train wreck nearby (the worst accident in the history of Amtrak), he worked nonstop from the Sunday afternoon when it happened until the following Tuesday morning. He was on the air almost the whole time. That's a long time to stay focused and prepared (not to mention awake and alert).

A PIECE OF HISTORY
He's also been part of history in the making. When Pope John Paul II came to Baltimore on a visit, he served as the radio pool coordinator. That meant that he provided the news to networks all over the world. It was a unique historical event, probably the only time in Miller's lifetime that the pope will

come to his city. He was there, watched it happen, and got a unique behind-the-scenes look at the entire event.

THANK YOU!
His junior high and high school English teachers played a big part in preparing Miller for what he is doing now. They encouraged him to excel in literature. They helped him hone his writing skills and put him on the path to seeking out news.

MILLER'S RECIPE FOR A GOOD REPORTER
Good reporters have to have perseverance, patience, and dedication. The job is fast-paced, demanding, and quite frankly, lots of hard work. Only a few people have the talent to be a good reporter. Fewer still are willing to work as hard as it takes to succeed. But the rewards are great.

Politician

WHAT IS A POLITICIAN?

Politicians are the people who have been chosen through an election process to govern a very specific geographical area—be it a small town, a state, or an entire nation. Most politicians are affiliated with a political party. The United States is currently a two-party system of Democrats and Republicans. Each party is based on mutual agreement on a platform of important issues. Each party chooses candidates for each election and backs them with time, finances, and other forms of support to help them win.

In a system based on the premise of government by the people, of the people, and for the people, there are a few hard and fast rules about who can run for an elected position. The basics include some age restrictions (for example, you must be at least 35 to run for president), U.S. citizenship, and other residency requirements. More often than not, those who are elected to political office are fairly well educated; however, a politician's educational background can run anywhere from political science and law to agronomy and education.

Probably, the single most important trait for a politician is to have the so-called fire in the belly—the drive and sense of purpose necessary to pursue political goals in spite of very challenging circumstances. A tradition of commitment and service to one's community and political party can also make a difference on election day.

Behind every politician—the winners and the losers—is a staff of political professionals, who are both paid and unpaid. There

are any number of clerks, campaign managers, press officers, media managers, research assistants, bill writers, speech writers, pages, and runners. These types of jobs provide an avenue for others with a desire to be involved in the political process without actually running for office themselves. Working as a "public servant" at any number of government agencies—on the local, state, or federal levels—is another means to serve one's country and make a difference.

 **TRY IT OUT**

RUN, RUN, RUN

Get involved in your own school politics. Run for student council (or form one if your school doesn't have one). If you aren't ready or interested in running yourself, volunteer to serve as campaign manager for another worthy candidate.

Make an official plan detailing how you hope to get yourself or your candidate elected. Include ideas for posters, outlines for speeches, and other materials that will help get your ideas across to your voters.

CAMPAIGN CITY

Volunteer to work on a political campaign in your area, whether for a mayoral candidate or a school board candidate. If someone in your town is running for a state or federal position, such as senator, volunteer to help with that campaign.

There is always plenty of work to be done—everything from stuffing envelopes to putting out posters. Make it a point to spend time with the experienced campaigners and watch what they do to run a campaign. Keep samples of all the campaign materials (for your candidate and the opponent) and note which tactics are most effective.

Look in the phone book for the Democratic or Republican headquarters in your town. Call them and see how you can help.

A LAW IS BORN

After all the speeches are made and the votes are counted, a politician's job has just begun. The following ideas will help you find out what a politician does during a typical day.

- ☼ Sit in on a school board meeting or town council meeting. Note the pros and cons of each issue being discussed.
- ☼ Take a tour of your state capitol during the legislative session. Sit in the visitors' gallery and listen to issues being debated in the Senate and House.
- ☼ Make an appointment to visit with your state or national senator or representative.
- ☼ Follow an issue by keeping track of its coverage in the local newspaper. Clip every article you can find about the process and keep notes on the details.
- ☼ Find an issue that you really believe in and become an advocate on its behalf. Writing letters, getting signatures on petitions, organizing activities to gain public attention, and speaking out in appropriate ways are all part of the process of getting good laws passed and bad laws repealed.

✔ CHECK IT OUT

🖱 ON THE WEB

ONLINE POLITICS

The following Web sites get the vote as kid-friendly places for kids to learn more about government:

- ☼ Ben's Guide to Government for Kids at http://bensguide
  .gpo.gov

- ☀ First Gov for Kids at http://www.kids.gov
- ☀ The White House for Kids http://www.whitehouse .gov/kids
- ☀ Kids in the House at http://clerkkids.house.gov
- ☀ Young Democrats of America at http://www.yda.org
- ☀ Young Republicans at http://www.youngrepublicans .com

📚 AT THE LIBRARY

GOVERNMENTAL BOOKSTOPS

Find out more about how the American political process works in books such as:

Burgan, Michael. *Creation of the U.S. Constitution.* New York: Capstone, 2006.

David, Kenneth. *Don't Know Much About the Presidents.* New York: Harper Collins, 2003.

Fradin, Dennis Brindell. *Declaration of Independence.* New York: Benchmark, 2006.

Panchyk, Richard. *Our Supreme Court: A History With 14 Activities.* Chicago: Chicago Review Press, 2006.

Small David. *So You Want to be President?* New York: Penguin, 2004.

Sobel, Syl. *The U.S. Constituion and You.* Hauppauge, N.Y.: 2001.

🗣 WITH THE EXPERTS

American Political Science Association
1527 New Hampshire Avenue NW
Washington, DC 20036-1206
http://www.apsanet.org

Democratic National Committee
430 South Capitol Street SE
Washington, DC 20003-4024
http://www.democrats.org

International City/County Management Association
777 North Capitol Street NE, Suite 500
Washington, DC 20002-4290
http://www.icma.org

League of Women Voters of the United States
1730 M Street NW, Suite 1000
Washington, DC 20036-4508
http://www.lwv.org

National Conference of State Legislatures
7700 East First Place
Denver, CO 80230-4207
http://www.ncsl.org

Republican National Committee
310 First Street SE
Washington, DC 20003-1885
http://www.gop.com

GET ACQUAINTED

Gail S. Schoettler, Politician

CAREER PATH

CHILDHOOD ASPIRATION: To learn all she could about everything.

FIRST JOB: Working cattle on her family's ranch.

CURRENT JOB: Political and business consultant.

A POLITICAL CAREER

Several years ago when Gail Schoettler was lieutenant governor of the state of Colorado, it wasn't at all unusual for her to give two to four speeches every day! She learned fast that if you want to be a politician, you have to be prepared to speak in front of groups of people—with or without advance preparation. Through the years, this skill, which she admits was something she had to learn, has served her well in many different positions.

It certainly helped during her campaign when she ran for governor and spent months criss-crossing the state speaking to voters. It also helped after she lost the election (something that sometimes happens to even the best politicians!) and was appointed by President Bill Clinton as U.S. Ambassador to the 2000 World Radiocommunication Conference (WRC) held in Istanbul. The assignment required her to lead a delegation of 162 U.S. telecommunications experts in a treaty negotiation with 189 countries on the allocation of radio spectrum for commercial and government uses. The stakes were high and the issues very complex, so Schoettler spent three months at the White House, six months at the State Department, and lots of time traveling all over the world learning how she could best represent U.S. interests. At the conference Schoettler met with representatives from many different countries in an effort to build support for the U.S. position. It took a lot of work by a lot of people, some very tough (and sometimes contentious) negotiations, but under Schoettler's leadership the U.S. team won everything they wanted.

After this success, Schoettler was asked to head the U.S. Defense Department's presidential transition for global intelligence, security, communications, and information technology, another important job that put often put her communication skills to the test.

BUILDING BRIDGES
One of the highlights of Schoettler's years as lieutenant governor was the opportunity to deal with many different issues and problems. At one point, she was a co-chair for the Summit of Eight conference held in Denver. (The Summit of Eight was an important meeting that brought the heads of

eight nations together to discuss international issues.) This meant she had to be sure things ran smoothly, and she had to greet the president of the United States, his counterparts from seven other countries, as well as all kinds of diplomats, press people, and other VIPs. She also had to be aware of the cultural values each person brought to the summit and the issues they found most important. Building bridges between the people and their opinions about the issues was the toughest part of the process for Schoettler. Reaching a point where everyone agrees on a solution takes a lot of hard work, but the end result makes it well worth the effort.

BE TRUE TO YOURSELF
The most important value to Schoettler is honesty. A politician and businessperson often has to make unpopular decisions. At times like that, Schoettler says that it's important to be true to your own principles and values. Even if the decision isn't popular or if someone disagrees, you need to stand by your decision and do what you think is right.

POLITICAL ROLE MODELS
No politician gets to the top without someone to help and guide them. Schoettler has found this guidance in many places. The governor has helped her with advice and direction. She also admires John F. Kennedy for his ability to inspire an entire generation and Eleanor Roosevelt for her political instincts and her role as first lady of the United States. She suggests that you find out all you can about Eleanor Roosevelt and how her work influenced an earlier generation of Americans.

Once, as a result of her leadership in the International Women's Forum, she was asked to give a speech in South Africa, where she met another of her political heroes, former South African President Nelson Mandela. She says that, in spite of facing horrible adversity, he is one of the few people on earth who is able to put bitterness aside for the benefit of his people.

Now she practices what she preaches as a political role model herself. She is part of an organization that raises money to help women get elected to Congress and as state governors. She also helps young women running for local offices in Colorado.

CLIMB YOUR MOUNTAINS

One of Schoettler's proudest recent accomplishments is that she climbed all 56 of Colorado's 14,000ers (mountains that are at least 14,000 feet high). This is an especially brave feat, since Schoettler is afraid of heights. But, she says, the climbs were something she really wanted to do, so she figured out a way to make it work in spite of her fear.

It's a strategy that will work for future politicians too—even those who are terrified of public speaking. She says to take on the challenges that scare you most. The more you do it, the better you'll get and the more confident you'll become.

Publicist

SKILL SET

✔ ART

✔ TALKING

✔ WRITING

GO to a major event in your town (a concert, sporting event, or movie premiere), and look at all promotional materials—news ads, feature stories, posters, and other promotions.

READ the lifestyles feature section of a major newspaper. Many of the articles you'll find there are the result of a publicist's efforts in promoting a client or a product.

TRY helping to promote the next school dance or sporting event.

WHAT IS A PUBLICIST?

Movie stars have them, major sports figures have them, politicians rely on them, and so does virtually every major corporation, government agency, nonprofit organization, and school. Publicists, also called public relations specialists (PR specialist, for short), help build a positive public image for all of these entities. They do this by generating publicity for their clients.

In an ideal situation, the publicity revolves around something good that has happened. For instance, a publicist might help a movie star promote a new movie or a corporation launch a new product. But publicists also have to be ready to respond to negative publicity about their client as well. This might involve some sort of tragedy or a big blunder on the part of their client. They have to be prepared, often at a moment's notice, to put a positive spin on even the worst of circumstances.

One of the earliest and still most famous business promoters was P.T. Barnum (of Barnum & Bailey Circus fame). He once said, "There is no such thing as bad publicity." A good publicist makes this statement true for his or her clients.

In order to promote their clients, publicists develop public relations campaigns that involve tasks such as writing press releases, organizing media conferences, designing brochures

and other promotional publications, and booking clients on radio and television talk shows. Three important details can determine the success of a public relations campaign. First is the newsworthiness of the information being presented. If a press release, for example, is simply a blatant advertisement for the client, it may not work. The PR specialist must develop angles or hooks that meet the needs of each media source's audience. This makes for a winning situation for both sides. The PR specialist gets the exposure, and the media source scores points for sharing interesting information with their readers.

The second aspect of a successful PR campaign is that the publicist has done the homework required and has produced top-notch materials. The media receives mountains of press packets every day. It takes some ingenuity to get one seen, let alone read, by a harried reporter.

The third key to a successful PR campaign is developing positive, personal relationships with media representatives. Such a relationship is achieved over time by producing consistent quality work and building a trustworthy reputation. Once that point is reached, reporters know to consider information that a specific publicist sends.

Sometimes people get public relations mixed up with marketing or advertising. Although the goals of both efforts are often similar, the methods are completely different. For one thing, publicity is free. Advertising costs big bucks.

There is a catch, of course. With publicity there is no guarantee that the media will "bite" and carry the story, and even if they do, there is no telling how they'll present the pitch. With advertising, you get exactly what you pay for and have complete control over how the message is conveyed.

To become a publicist requires a college degree with a major in public relations, journalism, advertising, or communications. To actually break into the field, experience in television, radio, or print journalism is often required. Some corporations will also want a publicist to have knowledge of the company's industry as well, although this can often be learned on the job.

Potential publicists should take advantage of every opportunity to get their name and work in print. A well-rounded, professional portfolio full of published articles, multimedia presentations, and other publications can open important career-enhancing doors.

P. T. Barnum summed up the role of publicists nicely when he said, "Without publicity a terrible thing happens—*nothing.*"

☞ TRY IT OUT

WHAT'S IN IT FOR ME?

Publicists are continually reminded that unless the audience has an interest in what they have to say, there will be no audience. Consumers want to know, "What's in it for me?"

Look at any good advertisement (key word here is *good*) to see this principle at work. Go through a magazine or newspaper and cut out three or four advertisements. See if you can identify the key benefits aimed at interesting you, the audience. For instance, does it mention things such as saving you money or improving your life? Mind you, just because the ad seems to promise miraculous results, doesn't mean that it's true. Beware of hype!

SPIN A TALE

This is a two-part project. First, take a trip to the library. Find out all you can about Benedict Arnold (he was a U.S. general who was considered a traitor during the Revolutionary War). Then, pretend that you are his PR person. What kind of spin could you put on his alleged betrayal that would get him off the hook?

Prepare a press kit containing your response. Make sure to include information about his background and a press release containing all the who, what, where, when, how, and why details that you can to try to save his neck.

THE BAD NEWS SPIN

One thing good publicists learn to do is make bad news sound —well—not so bad. Of course, there's a fine line between "spinning" the truth and telling an outright lie, and the best publicists learn not to cross it. Think of a bad-news situation you've heard about recently.

Write three different headlines for a story about the situation: one that just comes right out with the awful truth, one that truthfully spins the situation in a positive way, and one that colors the truth in what could easily be said to be a dishonest way. It's tricky, isn't it?

✔ CHECK IT OUT

🖱 ON THE WEB
PR ONLINE

Go online to learn more about working with the media:

- ☼ Take a virtual stroll through the Museum of Public Relations at http://www.prmuseum.com.
- ☼ See what a successful public relations campaign looks like at http://www.prsa.org/_Awards/silver/index.asp?ident=silO.
- ☼ Visit the White House newsroom at http://www.whitehouse.gov/news to see firsthand examples of a publicist's work.

☼ Think of a favorite company such as Gatorade (http://gatorade.com/press) or the Walt Disney Company (http://corporate.disney.go.com/news/corporate/2006/index0.html) and check out the latest news.
☼ Get the scoop on all your favorite stars at Teen People (http://www.teenpeople.com) and, yep, you better believe a publicist was hard at work behind all the headlines, good and bad.

📚 AT THE LIBRARY

SPEAK UP!
Find your voice and let it be heard with ideas discovered in books such as:

Cooper, Scott. *Speak Up and Get Along!* Minneapolis: Free Spirit, 2005.

Haugen, David. *Speechmakers and Writers.* Farmington Hills, Mich.: Thomson Gale, 2004.

Lombardi, Kristine. *Girls Talk: Complete Guide to IM Lingo, Emotions and More.* New York: Readers Digest, 2006.

Murphy, Thomas J. *What! I Have to Give a Speech?* Bloomington, Ind.: Family Learning Association, 2002.

Roy, Jennifer Rozines. *You Can Write Speeches and Debate.* New York: Enslow, 2003.

🗣 WITH THE EXPERTS

American Marketing Association
311 South Wacker Drive, Suite 5800
Chicago, IL 60606-6629
http://www.marketingpower.com

Promotion Marketing Association of America, Inc.
257 Park Avenue South, Floor 11
New York, NY 10010-7304
http://www.pmalink.org

Public Relations Society of America, Inc.
33 Maiden Lane, 11th Floor
New York, NY 10038-5150
http://www.prsa.org

GET ACQUAINTED

Rita Tateel

CAREER PATH

CHILDHOOD ASPIRATION: To be an actress.

FIRST JOB: Baby-sitting.

CURRENT JOB: President of The Celebrity Source, a celebrity recruitment agency.

FOR A GOOD CAUSE

Over the years, Rita Tateel has worked with thousands of celebrities. Her company, The Celebrity Source, matches stars wanting publicity or a chance to do a good deed with corporations or good causes looking to get attention for their products, events, or issues. Businesses use her services to find famous corporate spokespeople and to lend star power (and attract media attention) to their special events. Nonprofit organizations ask her to find celebrities willing to lend their names and cache to all kinds of causes, issues, and fund-raising events. Even government agencies call on her to find just the right person when they need a grand marshal for a parade or someone to attract interest at civic events. It can be a golf tournament or a movie premiere, a marketing campaign or a major fund-raiser—when people want celebrities, they call Tateel.

Whether they found fame and fortune in Hollywood, in fashion or the music industry, in a corporate board room, or even on a sports field, it's likely that Tateel has encountered them at some point during her over 20 years in the business. The list of those she has worked with looks like a who's who of celebrities and includes everyone from astronaut Buzz Aldrin and sports legend Muhammad Ali to media superstar Oprah Winfrey and movie stars Will Smith and George Clooney.

THE A-LIST

Yes, Tateel's work can be exciting, and yes, at times, it is very glamorous. But it also involves a lot of hard work and flawless communication skills. It can even get a bit stressful at times. Her work involves high-powered clients and big-name stars, all of whom are used to having what they want, how they want it, when they want it. It takes a lot of finesse and some fancy footwork to keep everyone happy.

Tateel describes a typical recruitment process as having several steps. First, a client contacts her and tells her what they need. Then she goes to her database of celebrity interests—lists are very important in her business—to come up with suitable suggestions. She takes the list back to the client and lets them pick their top choices. With their wish list in hand, Tateel and her colleagues set about trying to get the client the top celebrities on their list. This step isn't always as easy as it sounds. Tateel spends a lot of time coming up with the best strategy for approaching the celebrity. Sometimes they create a custom invitation and have it hand-delivered or send a carefully worded e-mail. Other times a simple phone call to the celebrity's agent or personal assistant will do the trick.

Once they get a yes, the real work begins! Her office often handles the celebrity's travel details and other logistics. They make sure that both the client and the celebrity know what they need to know about each other to feel comfortable in their roles. Most of the time, Tateel or others from her staff actually attend the celebrity events to make sure that everything goes smoothly and that the celebrity's needs are met. Tateel's continued success in the business depends on providing trustworthy service and exceptional attention to every detail.

THAT STAR QUALITY

Tateel majored in social work and child development in college. After she started working with celebrities, she thought that all her education would be useless. But she was wrong.

She was surprised to find that her strong background in psychology helps her understand how people think and why they act the way the do. This knowledge helps her build trust and rapport with even the most difficult people. It also helps keep her from getting star-struck and tongue-tied when working with the rich and famous.

Tateel admits that her business is a bit unusual. Many of the bigger public relations firms keep celebrity specialists in-house, while others focus on representing entertainment interests and individual celebrities. But very few share the special niche of celebrity-event recruitment that Tateel has successfully carved out for her company.

No matter what the emphasis of a publicist's work, Tateel says it is a great field for talkers. Tateel has a secret about what it takes to be a good talker too. She says that, in order to be a good talker, people need to do three things:

- ☼ They need to read a lot.
- ☼ They need to learn how to write in ways that other people can clearly understand.
- ☼ They need to know what's going on in the world.

Start with the smaller "worlds" of your school and community and broaden to the big events happening in your state, the country, and across the globe.

Retailer

WHAT IS A RETAILER?

People everywhere make a regular habit of buying things. Food, clothes, books, furniture, tools—you name it and someone wants to buy it. Retailers are the people who work in the stores that sell products for public consumption.

Retail stores come in all shapes and sizes. Some are independently owned and operated by someone as a private business. Sometimes called "mom and pop" businesses, these stores usually specialize in a particular type of merchandise, such as sports equipment or flowers. Other stores are franchises or branches of a major corporation. There are many fast-food chains that fall into this category. Another kind of retailer is a big department store. Then there are the more upscale shopping mall stores that specialize primarily in clothing and accessories as well as the superstores that carry a little bit of almost everything.

Big or little, all retail stores rely on a competent sales staff and effective managers to succeed. The sales staff might include cashiers, courtesy clerks, stockroom workers, and sales floor assistants. Most of these positions are entry level and many are available as part-time jobs for high school and college students.

Working in a retail store is one way to get the experience needed to become a retail manager. Retail managers and store owners often wear more than one hat around the store. They supervise and schedule the sales staff and are responsible for inventory control, customer service complaints, and training programs. They are responsible for the overall success of the store.

In larger stores and chains, there are several levels of management with the department manager being the first rung on the career ladder. In a big store, the store manager is in charge of the department managers and sets the policies and programs that guide the store. Higher up the ladder may be district, area, or regional managers who are responsible for more than one store.

As one might expect, the higher up the ladder you go, the more training you'll need. Most managers begin their careers working as part of the retail sales staff. In some cases, the store itself provides comprehensive training that might last from one week to a year or more. Other stores hire only management with a college-level degree in a business-related area such as business administration or marketing.

Two other professions associated with the retail industry are manufacturer's representatives (or reps) and buyers. The manufacturer's rep actually represents a specific manufacturer and the products it pro-
duces. Be it sports shoes or perfume, these people typically work in a specific "territory" and travel around to service established accounts and set up new ones. The person they are most likely to deal with at a larger store is the buyer. Buyers are responsible for choosing the merchandise that is sold in the store. This requires an accurate sense of what the store's customers will want to buy.

No matter what your ultimate ambition, if you are interested in a retailing career, a good place to start is with a high school cooperative education program. These programs provide an opportunity to earn while you gain firsthand experience in the business.

Overall, competition for customers in the retail industry can be as fierce as it is thrilling. There is always another way a customer can spend that dollar. A retailer's main mission is to find customers and keep them coming back for more.

 # TRY IT OUT

WARDROBE SHOPPING SPREE

Imagine that you have just won a $500 gift certificate at your favorite store. Use an Internet search engine such as http://www.google.com or http://www.yahoo.com to find the store's Web site. Then browse through the online catalog to put together a new (imaginary!) wardrobe. Print pictures of your favorite items and use them to create a catalog of your new look. Make sure to keep track of your virtual purchases so you'll know when you've tapped out your make-believe gift certificate.

CLEAN OUT THE GARAGE!

Ask your family what they think about getting rid of some of the excess clutter around your house. If they sound interested, team up with them to host a garage sale (also known as a yard sale, tag sale, etc.). Clean out your attic, your garage, your basement, and your bedroom.

Organize and price everything that you decide to sell. Arrange things on tables, racks, or in boxes. Make it as easy as possible to spot all the bargains. Make signs to advertise the event and consider placing a classified ad in the local paper. The better you get the word out, the more potential buyers you'll attract.

On the day of the event, be prepared with about $20 in change, a designated spot to keep the cash, and a notebook to keep track of each sale.

At the end of the day, tally up the sales and invite the whole family out for dinner to celebrate.

COMPARISON SHOPPER

Visit two or more stores that specialize in the same kinds of merchandise. Grocery stores, hardware stores, and discount department stores are some ideas to consider. Walk through the store and note how the departments and merchandise are displayed. List the three things you like best and the three things you like least about each store. While you are there, jot down the prices of several items. Find the same items in each store and compare the prices.

CHECK IT OUT

ON THE WEB

CYBER SHOPPING

Enjoy some fun virtual shopping experiences at Web sites such as:

- My Scene at http://myscene.everythinggirl.com/home.aspx
- General Mills Millsberry at http://www.millsberry.com/index.phtml
- Neopets at http://www.neopets.com

AT THE LIBRARY

FROM START TO FINISH

Find out how some of your favorite products get to market in these titles from the *Made in U.S.A.* series:

Blackbirch. *Made In U.S.A.: Cell Phones.* Farmington Hills, Mich.: Blackbirch, 2005.

————. *Made In U.S.A.: Pianos.* Farmington Hills, Mich.: Blackbirch, 2005.

Englhart, Mindi. *Made In U.S.A.: Bikes.* Farmington Hills, Mich.: Blackbirch, 2002.

————. *Made In U.S.A.: CDs.* Farmington Hills, Mich.: Black-birch, 2001.

————. *Made In U.S.A.: Cheese.* Farmington Hills, Mich.: Black-birch, 2005.

Smith, Ryan. *Made In U.S.A.: Golf Balls.* Farmington Hills, Mich.: Blackbirch, 2005.

Woods, Samuel. *Made In U.S.A.: Kid's Clothes.* Farmington Hills, Mich.: Blackbirch, 1999.

————. *Made In U.S.A.: Sneakers.* Farmington Hills, Mich.: Blackbirch, 1999.

WITH THE EXPERTS

American Management
  Association
1601 Broadway
New York, NY 10019-7434
http://www.amanet.org

Food Marketing Institute
655 15th Street, NW
Washington, DC 20005-5701
http://www.fmi.org

National Association of
  Convenience Stores
1600 Duke Street
Alexandria, VA 22314-3466
http://www.nacsonline.com

National Retail Federation
325 7th Street NW, 1100
Washington, DC 20004
http://www.nrf.com

GET ACQUAINTED

Diana Nelson, Retailer

ALL SYSTEMS RETAIL

Diana Nelson went to college in Chicago to study fashion merchandising, fully intending to head to New York City for a career as a fashion designer. By the time she graduated

CAREER PATH

CHILDHOOD ASPIRATION: To be the next big fashion designer.

FIRST JOB: Selling hot dogs at the local pool.

CURRENT JOB: Owner of Kazoo and Company, an award-winning toy store in Denver, Colorado.

from college, completed her management training at a Marshall Fields department store, and pursued a retail career at the Gap, her plans had changed a bit.

When she took a road trip out to visit her old college roommate in Los Angeles, her plans changed even more. That's because she stopped in Denver, fell in love with the city, and never left. While there, her retail career took some interesting twists and turns when she accepted a position as the first female national account manager for Coors, a Fortune 500 company. Then she took a turn as marketing director at the Keystone Ski Resort.

Along the way she married, had two children, and went back to school to earn credentials as a neuromuscular therapist. She enjoyed a five-year practice as a therapist, and then life took another unexpected turn when Nelson found herself divorced and in need of a solid income to support her family. She decided that owning her own business offered the best chance for her to meet her financial goals and started researching different business opportunities. She discovered that Kazoo and Company, a popular toy store in Denver, was for sale and decided that it was a natural fit for a single mom with two small children.

EVERY DAY IS PLAY DAY

Nelson realizes that owning a toy store is like a dream come true for lots of kids and admits that she does spend a lot of time playing with the 60,000 different products her store sells. She says that being a single mom and a business owner requires her to run her life a little differently than other people do. The hours can get long and a little stressful, but she says you do what you have to do to take care of your family. The good thing for her boys, ages 9 and 11, is that they often get to go to work with Mom. She even lets them pick out toys to sell from time to time. And she always makes sure there is plenty of time to indulge their athletic interests in sports such as snowboarding, golf, and soccer!

Since she bought Kazoo, the company has grown and expanded in exciting ways. They now offer an online store (http://www.kazootoys.com) and send catalogs to their regular customers. The company must be doing something right, since they have been voted the number-one toy Internet site by *Playthings* magazine, the toy retailer of the year for several years running (they even beat out national chains like FAO Schwarz), and have been named one of the top five retailers in America. Nelson says the great customer service her store offers keeps people coming back for more.

ADVICE FOR SALE

Whether or not you decide to go into retail as a career, Nelson has some advice for you. She says that whatever you do, you want to be happy doing it. It comes down to making a life, making a living, and loving what you do. If you love what you do, the rest will come naturally. Plus, when you have fun doing what you're doing, the days go by very fast!

Social Worker

WHAT IS A SOCIAL WORKER?

Social workers and counselors listen to people, ask questions, and find useful resources to help people solve all kinds of problems. There's certainly no shortage of problems to deal with in this profession. Drug and alcohol addictions, child abuse, and homelessness are just a few of the challenges social workers have to face every day.

Some social workers specialize in helping people with emotional or mental problems. Others deal exclusively with children. Quite often this type of work involves helping someone who doesn't have anywhere else to turn. For instance, some social workers help people who are seriously ill with diseases such as AIDS find someone to take care of them or

connect them with a hospice. Counselors also specialize in dealing with certain types of problems such as injury rehabilitation, terminal illness, grief, marriage and family, and problem pregnancies.

One likely place to find a social worker is in a school just like yours. Here social workers help students deal with problems such as cutting classes, flunking out of school, or taking drugs. Other school counselors help students find just the right college for them.

Increasingly in demand are gerontological social workers. These social workers assist the elderly with things like finding transportation to doctor's appointments, nursing home care, and other services.

Yet another type of counseling involves helping people find or change their careers. You might even want to talk to one of these counselors in your search!

To become a social worker you must be licensed by the state in which you work and complete some very specific education. A bachelor's degree is a must and a minimum! If you want to work in any of the health-care fields, you will also need a master's degree. A doctorate is required if you want to teach social work at a college or university.

With so many problems in the world today, you can really take your pick of the area in which you want to work. Social work is all about helping people and families get along better. The work can be heartwarming, but sometimes it's heartbreaking. It takes a caring, strong person who's not afraid to deal with the best and worst life has to offer to succeed as a social worker.

☞ TRY IT OUT

WHAT IF...

What if one of your friends was in trouble with something big? Like homelessness, family violence, or something too big for them to handle by themselves. Where could they turn for help? First, make a list of all the trusted adults you could turn to for help and include a way to reach them at school, by e-mail, or by phone. Then take a look through the local phone book and online to identify programs that might be useful in a crisis. Write down each program's name, a brief description of their services, and contact information. Keep your list handy just in case.

JUST DO IT!

Now's the time to find out if a career in social work is right for you. Fortunately, there are plenty of opportunities to test your helping skills. Volunteer anywhere that you'll have a chance to meet people. This can include nursing homes, child-care centers, or food-delivery programs. Many elder-care homes have a need for people to just read and talk to the residents.

The benefits of volunteering are twofold. You can make a difference while you find out how you like working with people with problems.

If you need ideas about kinds of volunteer jobs, check out the following books:

Black, Michael. *Volunteering to Help Kids.* New York: Scholastic, 2006.
Clark, Sondra. *You Can Change Your World: Creative Ways to Volunteer and Make a Difference.* Nashville, Tenn.: Baker, 2003.
Isler, Claudia. *Volunteering to Help Animals.* New York: Scholastic, 2006.
Newell, Patrick. *Volunteering to Help Seniors.* New York: Scholastic, 2006.

For ideas about helping make the world a better place during your next family vacation, see:

McMillon, Bill. *Volunteer Vacations.* Chicago: Chicago Review Press, 1997.

PLAY DEAR ABBY

Every newspaper has at least one advice column. People write letters explaining their problem and the advice columnist gives them ideas on how to solve it.

Try your hand at the advice business with the help of your local newspaper and a roll of adhesive tape. First, find and cut out the advice column in the newspaper, but don't read it yet. Next, ask a friend or family member to tape bits of paper over all the advice columnist's answers so all you can see are the questions.

Now, read each question carefully and write an appropriate response. This part may involve some detective work! You may have to find out a little more about the problem before offering adequate advice. What resources are there that can help? This is where the Yellow Pages and the local library can come in handy.

Finally, take a look at the advice columnist's responses and see how your answers compare. (If you really get the hang of things, you might consider approaching your school newspaper with an offer to write an advice column for them.)

✔ CHECK IT OUT

🖱 ON THE WEB

DON'T JUST SIT THERE!

Social workers are problem solvers at heart. You don't have to wait until you are an adult to help other people. Following are some programs to investigate:

- ☼ Do Something at http://www.dosomething.org
- ☼ Speak up at http://www.kidscom.com/chat/vttw/voice_index.html
- ☼ Youth Service America at http://www.ysa.org
- ☼ Youth Venture at http://www.youthventure.org
- ☼ Explore the world with Peace Corps at http://www.peacecorps.gov/kids

📚 AT THE LIBRARY
WORKING ON SOLUTIONS
Find out more about the types of problems social workers try to solve in books such as:

Eubanks, Sonia. *Social Issues Firsthand: Death and Dying.* Farmington Hills, Mich.: Greenhaven, 2006.

George, Charles. *Social Issues Firsthand: Racism.* Farmington Hills, Mich.: Greenhaven, 2006.

Haugen, David. *Social Issues Firsthand: Adoption.* Farmington Hills, Mich.: Greenhaven, 2005.

Hill, Mary K. *Social Issues Firsthand: Prisons.* Farmington Hills, Mich.: Greenhaven, 2006.

———. *Social Issues Firsthand: Poverty.* Farmington Hills, Mich.: Greenhaven, 2006.

Richards, Linda. *Social Issues Firsthand: Family Violence.* Farmington Hills, Mich.: Greenhaven, 2006.

🗣 WITH THE EXPERTS
American Counseling Association
5999 Stevenson Avenue
Alexandria, VA 22304-3304
http://www.counseling.org

Council for Accreditation of Counseling and Related Educational Programs
5999 Stevenson Avenue
Alexandria, VA 22304-3304
http://www.cacrep.org

Council on Social Work Education
1725 Duke Street, Suite 500
Alexandria, VA 22314-3457
http://www.cswe.org

National Association of Social Workers
First Street NE, Suite 525
Washington, DC 20002-4241
http://www.socialworkers.org

National Association of Workforce Development Professionals
810 First Street NE, Suite 525
Washington, DC 20002-4227
http://www.nawdp.org

National Network for Social Work Managers, Inc.
1040 West Harrison Street
Chicago, IL 60607-7134
http://www.socialworkmanager.org

School Social Work Association of America
PO Box 2072
Northlake, IL 60614-0072
http://www.sswaa.org

GET ACQUAINTED

Deborah Alexander,
Social Worker

CAREER PATH

CHILDHOOD ASPIRATION: To be a nursery school teacher.

FIRST JOB: Baby-sitting and teaching guitar lessons.

CURRENT JOB: Licensed clinical social worker and supervisor at Family Service of Santa Monica.

AN EARLY START

Deborah Alexander found inspiration for her future career when she was in preschool. She remembers having wonderful preschool teachers—even though it's been well over 40 years since she was in their class! In fact, these people were so important to Alexander's family that her parents are still good friends with them. She recalls that they were such positive role models that she knew even then that she wanted to grow up to work with little children like they did.

When it came time to choose a college degree, however, Alexander chose to go with social work instead of early childhood development because she learned that it would prepare her for more options. She liked that she'd be qualified to work with children of all ages in a wide variety of settings. With more than 20 years experience in the field, Alexander is glad that she chose social work and continues to enjoy helping all kinds of people with all kinds of problems. She says that some times people are dealing with things going wrong in their lives and some need a little help getting used to things going right. For instance, some children need help getting through tough situations like divorce or domestic violence, while others may need some extra care getting used to potentially good situations such as going to a new school or welcoming a new brother or sister into their lives.

The agency where Alexander works helps individuals, couples, and families work through many different kind of issues, including anxiety, depression, marital relationships, the loss of a loved one, substance abuse, career changes, life transitions, illness and disability, separation and divorce, and parenting.

PLAY IT OUT

Maybe you've heard someone say that a good way to deal with problems is to "talk it out." That's always good advice, but in the case of some of Alexander's youngest clients (kids under the age of five), some of them just don't have the verbal skills to explain what's wrong and why they are upset. In those cases, Alexander uses play therapy to help them sort through their feelings. Her office is fully equipped with lots of dolls, puppets, art materials, building blocks, and other toys. She says that sometimes something as simple as letting a child bang wooden pegs with a play hammer can help them explain angry feelings.

Other times she might resort to a game of hide-and-seek to help a young child communicate their fears about going to preschool. Alexander lets the child take the lead by choosing a hiding spot and giving her clues about when to find him or her. This way the child starts to understand that he or she has some control over their feelings about separation and reunion with their mom. It's like they are able to explain the situation to someone who understands—by their actions in play, they can say "I get scared without Mommy and I want to see her again." Alexander says that her own calm reaction helps reassure the child that they can survive the situation. After "listening" to the child in this way, Alexander will work with the parents and the child's teacher to come up with ideas to help the child cope with his or her separation anxiety.

PROFESSIONAL SOUNDING BOARD
In addition to seeing clients, Alexander is responsible for supervising other social workers who are working toward meeting their licensing requirements. She says this is an important part of the social work model and credits it for preventing social workers from getting totally bummed out by all the bad situations they encounter. The supervisor provides support to the new social workers by helping them process their own feelings about the problems their client's are dealing with. Alexander says it always helps to have someone listen to you unload a little after a rough day.

SOCIAL WORKERS IN WAITING
One way to know if you're cut out to be a social worker is to notice if you enjoy helping other people, advises Alexander. She also says that if you can see things from another person's point of view and are curious about what it's like to walk in someone else's shoes, you've got two very important traits for a social worker to have.

Speech Pathologist

WHAT IS A SPEECH PATHOLOGIST?

Imagine life without the ability to speak or be understood. It changes even the most basic tasks in major ways. Since spoken words are the foundation for a person's ability to communicate, not being able to speak would alter a person's life in a huge way.

Speech pathologists work with people of all ages to help them use their voices to communicate clearly and effectively. This might involve working with a child born with a birth defect such as a cleft lip or one with developmental disabilities that result in having trouble producing sounds or being understood. It could involve helping someone who has damaged their vocal cords due to excessive use or has developed a voice disorder. Some speech pathologists work with patients who are recovering from illnesses such as strokes or head injuries to help them relearn vital communication skills. Others work with professionals who are trying to improve their diction and presentation skills or rid themselves of an obvious accent.

The work of speech pathologists usually consists of a three-step process. First, they must assess the nature of the problem. Speech pathologists use a variety of tests and special instruments to help them diagnose speech problems.

The second step involves therapy or treatment of the problem. This can be done on a one-on-one basis or with a small group. Speech pathologists draw from a wide array of activities and treatment plans to help correct various speech problems.

The final step is evaluation. In the best of circumstances, this step is used to determine when someone is completely rehabilitated and free of speech disorders. Other times it is used to gauge the effectiveness of the treatment plan and make necessary adjustments.

Audiologists could be considered "career cousins" to speech pathologists. What speech pathologists are to speech, audiologists are to hearing. They provide similar types of care to people with different needs. Sometimes their work intersects with one another, and they must team up to provide effective care. Put simply, audiology and speech pathology are about helping people hear and be heard.

Schools, clinics, hospitals, rehabilitation centers, and research centers are typical places where both audiologists and speech pathologists might work. Both jobs reflect a unique blend of both the education and health-care fields.

In order to meet certification requirements of the American Speech, Language, and Hearing Associations, practicing speech pathologists must earn a master's degree in speech-language pathology or audiology. While a master's is considered the standard credential in this field, some states allow people with a bachelor's degree to work under special supervision with students in schools.

☞ TRY IT OUT

ACT THE PART
Drama can be an enjoyable way to enhance your speaking skills because you have to slip into someone else's voice and mannerisms in order to act different parts. Make a point of auditioning for the next school play. While you are learning your lines, make a conscious effort to improve your enunciation, diction, and projection skills. Your drama coach will be more than happy to help you achieve these goals.

WALK IN THEIR SHOES
Sometimes when something comes easily for you, it is hard to understand why it's so difficult for someone else. In order to be effective, speech pathologists must be able to understand the frustration that their clients feel at not being able to communicate.

For a quick lesson in empathy, check out some foreign language tapes from the library or video store. Listen to a short dialogue segment several times until you think you can repeat what is being said. Keep trying until you get it right. Use a tape recorder to keep track.

The focus, the failure, the frustration you may feel at trying to make these foreign sounds are precisely what some people feel just trying to say hello in their own language.

ON THE JOB
Imagine that you are a speech pathologist and your first patient is a child who stutters. Learn more about what's it like to be a child who stutters at the National Stuttering Association Web site at http://www.nsastutter.org. Another professional organization to investigate is the Stuttering Foundation at http://www.stuttersfa.org. Use the information you find there to make a list of five tips to share with your young patient.

✔ CHECK IT OUT

🖱 ON THE WEB

SPEECH THERAPY TOOLBOX

Go online to experiment with some of the activities and games speech pathologists use to help their young patients:

- ☼ Juniors Web at http://www.juniorsweb.com/slp/index .asp
- ☼ Sequencing Fun at http://www.quia.com/pages/ sequencingfun.html
- ☼ I Love Speech and Language at http://www.quia .com/pages/havefun.html
- ☼ And find links to all kinds of speech and language games and activities at http://www.angelfire.com/ nj/speechlanguage/Onlineactivities.html

📚 AT THE LIBRARY

TONGUE TRIPS

Have some fun mastering the tongue twisters featured in books that include:

Artell, Mike. *Ten-Second Tongue Twisters*. New York: Sterling, 2006.

Cobb, Rebecca. *Tongue Twisters to Tangle Your Tongue*. New York: Marion Boyars, 2005.

Rosenberg, Pam. *Tongue Twisters*. Minneapolis: Child's World, 2004.

Rosenbloom, Joseph. *Giggle Fit: Tricky Tongue Twisters*. New York: Sterling, 2002.

Tait, Chris. *Ridiculous Tongue Twisters*. New York: Sterling, 2005.

🗣️ WITH THE EXPERTS

American Academy of Audiology
11730 Plaza America Drive, Suite 300
Reston, VA 20190-4748
http://www.americanboardofaudiology.org

American Speech Language-Hearing Association
10801 Rockville Pike
Rockville, MD 20852-3226
http://www.asha.org

National Student Speech Language Hearing Association
10801 Rockville Pike
Rockville, MD 20852-3226
http://www.nsslha.org

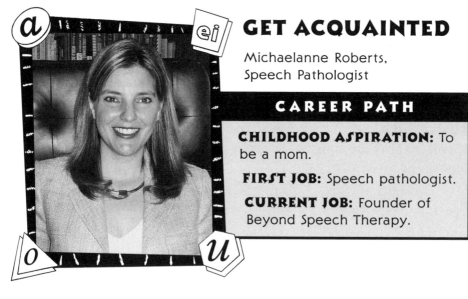

GET ACQUAINTED

Michaelanne Roberts,
Speech Pathologist

CAREER PATH

CHILDHOOD ASPIRATION: To be a mom.

FIRST JOB: Speech pathologist.

CURRENT JOB: Founder of Beyond Speech Therapy.

DAD WAS RIGHT!

When Michaelanne Roberts left for college, her dad gave her some advice: Find something you love to do and you'll be successful. By the end of her freshman year, she knew she wanted to do something to help people and spent the summer visiting different businesses to get some ideas. One of the places she visited was a hospital-based speech pathology clinic that offered a program called Easy Street. Easy Street simulates typical community settings where patients recovering from stroke, arthritis, traumatic brain injury, orthopedic surgery, or other life-changing disabilities can relearn skills needed for daily living. She, like most people, didn't realize how challenging it could be for a person to have to learn basic skills like walking, talking, and eating and recognized immediately that she had found a helping career she could love.

Back at college, she worked toward a degree in speech pathology. Like most licensed speech pathologists, her training included four years of college, one to two years of graduate school, and a nine-month clinical fellowship. At that point she had to take and pass a national exam and apply for a license. Then, and only then, was she qualified to sign her name with the added distinction of CCC/SLP (which stands for Certificate of Clinical Competence/Speech and Language Pathology).

SOMETHING MISSING
Roberts started her career working as a speech pathologist with head-injury and stroke patients in a rehabilitation center. Her job was to evaluate their needs and determine treatment plans that would allow them to function as effectively as possible in spite of their injuries. However, because of insurance rules, she soon discovered that many of her patients had to be discharged from care before they were better. This was not what she had in mind when she set out to help people, and she decided to do something about it.

Instead of giving in to the problem, Roberts started thinking about better solutions. The result? She asked herself, "What kinds of skills do people need to succeed in their life and work?" Then she started a company where she could create tools that patients could use on their own to continue treatment at home. Now her computer-based therapy programs are used in schools, hospitals, clinics, and even corporations to help people with a variety of speech problems.

For instance, school-based speech pathologists teach parents and teachers how to use one of Roberts's programs to help students who have speech and language problems. Hospitals show stroke and head-injury patients and their families how to use a special program at home to practice skills they learn in rehab. Corporations use another program to help people learn how to speak English clearly and without accents.

Now, instead of getting just an hour or so of care per week with a professional, the people using Robert's programs can get several hours of practice. And, since speech pathology is one of those areas where practice makes perfect, these patients achieve much greater success in overcoming their difficulties. Speech pathology professionals can focus their attention on evaluating the patient's strengths and weaknesses and making treatment plans. And patients get the treatment they need to get better and back in the thick of life.

And it's all possible because Roberts saw a problem and came up with solution. Now that's helping people!

A WORD FOR FUTURE SPEECH PATHOLOGISTS

Roberts believes that speech pathology is a great field that offers a fascinating variety of opportunities. Depending on what they like best, speech pathologists can work in hospitals, schools, private practice, or even corporations. She is excited to think about the many ways that technology can be used to help provide cost-effective ways to deliver therapy. She hopes that you'll find out, like she did, that her dad was right—do something that you love and success will follow.

Sports Professional

SHORTCUTS

SKILL SET

✔ TALKING

✔ SPORTS

✔ BUSINESS

GO take a class at a health and fitness club.

READ *Tiger Woods: Sports Heroes and Legends* by Matt Doeden (Minneapolis: Lerner, 2005).

TRY teaching a friend how to play your favorite game.

WHAT IS A SPORTS PROFESSIONAL?

A successful sports professional, or pro, has to be good enough to wow seasoned athletes and patient enough to teach first-time players. Sports pros work at resorts or clubs and teach a particular sport such as golf, tennis, swimming, or skiing.

Sports pros can work with individuals or groups, children or adults. They must be able to instruct, evaluate, and advise both beginners and experts on ways to improve their game or skills. A training session with a sports pro generally consists of three parts: a demonstration of the required skills, an explanation of the rules, and an overview of basic safety precautions. After that it's practice, practice, and more practice on specific skills.

Communication skills and the ability to get along with others are just as important as athletic ability in this people-oriented business. Sports pros have to keep their students motivated to work hard and challenged to push themselves to improve.

Training other trainers is often part of the job for the more experienced sports pro. Other advanced opportunities for sports pros include running the administrative side of a training program or supervising other instructors.

Other types of sports such as diving, hiking, and cycling lend themselves to other types of ventures for sports pros (and fanatics). Organizing tours and special trips for beginners and more advanced learners is another way to earn a living by teaching others how to play.

Becoming a personal trainer who designs personalized fitness programs for individual people is another route to follow. Taking into consideration a person's fitness level, eating habits, and overall lifestyle, a trainer creates a personalized workout plan and helps clients stick to it.

The best training anyone can get to be a sports pro is to master one's sport. Needless to say, a golf pro must be an excellent golfer, and a ski instructor must be a great skier. It is essential that sports pros have good communication skills, and it really helps if they genuinely enjoy working with people. Focus, concentration, and massive amounts of patience also come in handy when training other people.

☞ TRY IT OUT

JOIN THE CLUB

The best advice for would-be sports pros: If your game is hockey, play hockey; if your sport is tennis, play tennis; etc. If your school has a team or club for any of these sports, join it. Learn all you can.

Remember, you have to be very good at your sport to be a sports pro. Enter tournaments and contests. Play the tour. The more you play, the better you get. The better you get, the easier it is to help others.

COPYCAT

As the saying goes, "Imitation is the sincerest form of flattery." While you may have to face the fact that you'll never be the next Venus Williams or Tiger Woods, you can learn to apply some of their best traits to your own sports career.

First, make a list of your favorite sports heroes. Leave space for comments under each name. Next, think about the traits that make these people so successful. Is it their focus? Their persistence and dedication? Finally, describe these special traits in the space beneath each name. Determine to do whatever it takes to be a copycat in some of these important areas.

✔ CHECK IT OUT

🖱 ON THE WEB

WALKING SPORTS ENCYCLOPEDIA

Part of a sports pro's job is to keep students entertained. Since the pro and the student share a common interest in the sport, keep up with what's happening and who's doing what so that you'll always have plenty to talk about.

For the computer-literate, there are a growing number of information resources and forums on the Internet. Following are addresses for a few general sources.

ONLINE SPORTS

Learn the rules of the sports game at these Web sites:

- ☀ Catch the latest news from *Sports Illustrated for Kids* at http://www.sikids.com.
- ☀ Find links to all kinds of sports Web sites at http://www.northvalley.net/kids/sports.shtml.

☀ Find even more links to sports stuff online at http://cybersleuth-kids.com/sleuth/Sports.
☀ Another big sports site with lots of links can be found at http://school.discovery.com/schrockguide/popspt.html.

THE NUMBER GAME

Have fun testing your skill at all kinds of sports trivia and statistics at these Web sites:

☀ NFL's Play Football at http://www.playfootball.com/games
☀ Time for Kid's Olympics at http://www.timeforkids.com/TFK/olympics
☀ Sports Illustrated for Kids at http://www.sikids.com

And for a whomping list of sports trivia online, go to http://www.primate.wisc.edu/people/hamel/sportstriv.html.

AT THE LIBRARY

SPORTS PRO IN TRAINING

Find out more about how to play your favorite sports in books such as:

Crisfield, Deborah. *The Everything Kids Soccer Book: Rules, Techniques and More About Your Favorite Sport.* Boston: Adams Media, 2002.

Eule, Brian. *Basketball for Fun.* Mankato, Minn.: Capstone, 2003.

Gordon, John. *The Kids' Book of Golf.* Tonawanda, N.Y.: Kids Can, 2001.

Gruber, Brian. *Gymnastics for Fun.* Mankato, Minn.: Capstone, 2004.

Rossiter, Sean. *Hockey: How to Play Like the Pros.* Vancouver, B.C.: Douglas & McIntyre, 2004.

Thomas, Keltic. *How Baseball Works*. Toronto, Ont.: Maple Tree, 2004.
———. *How Basketball Works*. Toronto, Ont.: Maple Tree, 2005.
———. *How Hockey Works*. Toronto, Ont.: Maple Tree, 2002.
Will, Sandra. *Hockey for Fun*. Mankato, Minn.: Capstone, 2003.
———. *Lacrosse for Fun*. Mankato, Minn.: Capstone, 2006.
Willett, Andrew. *Swimming for Fun*. Mankato, Minn.: Capstone, 2003.

🗣< WITH THE EXPERTS

American Alliance for Health, Physical Education, Recreation and Dance
1900 Association Drive
Reston, VA 20191
http://www.aahperd.org

Ladies Professional Golf Association
100 International Golf Drive
Daytona Beach, FL 32124-1092
http://www.lpga.com

National Athletic Trainers Association
2952 Stemmons Freeway
Dallas, TX 75247-6113
http://www.nata.org

National PGA Tour Office
112 PGA TOUR Boulevard
Ponte Verde, FL 32082
http://www.pgatour.com

National Professional Golfers of America
100 Avenue of the Champions
Palm Beach Gardens, FL 33418
http://www.pga.com

Professional Ski Instructors of America
133 South Van Gordon, Suite 101
Lakewood, CO 80228-1706
http://www.psia.org

U.S. Golf Association
PO Box 708
Far Hills, NJ 07931-0708
http://www.usga.org

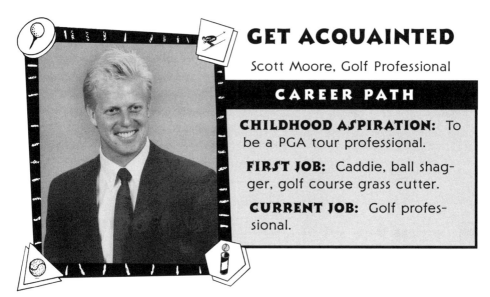

GET ACQUAINTED

Scott Moore, Golf Professional

CAREER PATH

CHILDHOOD ASPIRATION: To be a PGA tour professional.

FIRST JOB: Caddie, ball shagger, golf course grass cutter.

CURRENT JOB: Golf professional.

HE GETS PAID TO HAVE FUN

Scott Moore loves to play golf. It's been a passion of his since he was old enough to walk around the golf course. His dad was a golf pro, so Moore spent much of his childhood shagging balls and caddying. He learned the sport at an early age, and he lives and breathes it now. Sometimes he has to pinch himself to believe that he earns his living playing golf.

PEE-WEE SPECIAL

One of the most rewarding parts of his job is working with children, especially those who have never even seen a golf course before. Every Tuesday afternoon at 2:00, Moore introduces a new bunch of kids to the game. It's nice to see a child's face light up when he or she makes a good shot. He says some children are natural golfers, and he enjoys being part of turning them on to the sport.

A SPECIAL PERK OF THE JOB

The most treasured part of his job is the lifelong friendships that he's cultivated with many of his clients. Mutual trust is an important part of these special relationships.

In the course of an 18-hole game, there's plenty of time to talk. His clients often share details about their marriages,

132

their kids, their problems, and their hopes and dreams. He says he keeps things confidential and doesn't tell secrets. He likes being a sort of sounding board for ideas and feelings, as well as teaching a good game of golf.

IT'S A DEAL

Golf is a favorite sport of businesspeople everywhere. He says that sometimes he feels like a fly on the wall watching a big business deal come together during a round of golf. The give-and-take process can make for an interesting game.

WILDEST DREAMS

Moore never thought that he could go from being a golf pro at 24 years old to owning his own golf course at 34. But that's just what he did. In the process, he's added financing, inventory control, marketing, and personnel management to his job description. In spite of a few nightmarish aspects in the process, it's been a dream come true.

A FAMILY AFFAIR

Moore says that if he didn't have the support of his family, he wouldn't be able to do his job. He works long hours. He often leaves the house before his young children are up in the morning and doesn't get home until after they're in bed. His busiest times at work are during their school vacations and on weekends.

He makes a special effort to set time aside to be with his family. This helps, but it's nice to know they're behind him 100 percent.

FREE ADVICE

Moore has a few tips to help you improve your chances of success as a sports pro.

- ☼ Be prepared to put in long hours. (During the off-season he still works 50-hour weeks at his Alabama golf course.)
- ☼ Be prepared to really love what you do.
- ☼ Be patient. Some people gripe about everything and you'll have a difficult time pleasing everyone. But you'll make some great contacts.

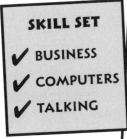

TAKE A TRIP!

Telemarketer

SHORTCUTS

SKILL SET

✔ BUSINESS
✔ COMPUTERS
✔ TALKING

GO browse through the technology equipment at an office supply store to see the newest kinds of gizmos available.

READ about avoiding telemarketing scams at http://www.state.sd.us/attorney/kidskorner/teen/telemarketing.htm.

TRY calling people in your school to remind them about a meeting or an assignment.

WHAT ARE TELEMARKETERS?

The invention of the telephone completely revolutionized the way people do business. With recent advances in modems, faxes, and e-mail, the telephone continues to have a major impact on all kinds of business.

A telemarketer typically calls hundreds of people every day in order to sell products and services over the phone. Telemarketers are used to get information to or from a group of people quickly and efficiently. Often automatic dialing systems are used. As soon as one call is done, the computer automatically dials another. So, it can mean constant (make that nonstop) telephone talking.

Telephones are so important to business that there are a number of specific telemarketing careers that revolve around using them almost exclusively.

Airline reservation agents work for a specific airline and help customers book flights. Using sophisticated computer programs, they check on the status of a flight, make seat assignments, and issue tickets.

A collection agent calls people who haven't paid their bills on time. His or her mission is to collect the money owed to the client. Contrary to popular opinion, these agents don't use strong-arm tactics to do this, just the telephone. They need to be firm with people and comfortable about asking for money. They can't take flimsy excuses or "no" for an answer.

There are several different kinds of dispatchers. One kind uses a telephone and a radio to make sure that taxis, rental trucks, trains, and other forms of ground transportation get to where they need to go. A police dispatcher will take emergency calls and relay them to the officers responding to each situation. An emergency (911) dispatcher might also send an ambulance, a fire crew, or a helicopter to the scene of an accident.

A customer service representative uses the telephone to talk to customers of a business. Representatives may fill orders or deal with complaints. Either way, they use the phone to keep customers happy.

A hotel desk clerk takes reservations from people calling in, directs calls from guests to the correct person, and forwards incoming calls to guests. Like a receptionist, the desk clerk is often a first contact with the hotel for some people. He or she may also be the person who processes guests in and out of the hotel.

A market researcher gathers information about products, lifestyles, habits, and choices—really just about anything anyone wants to know. A market researcher might make calls to find out how someone is likely to vote in the next election, what radio station they listen to, or what kind of soap they use in the laundry. The information that is gathered is compiled into reports that are used to help business leaders make decisions. For instance, if the information indicates that nobody is listening to their radio station, the company president would want to make some big changes.

A receptionist answers calls that come into an office and directs calls to the appropriate person or department. This may sound easy, but when you are answering 100 or more phone lines at once, it can get pretty hectic. Receptionists are usually stationed at the main entrance to the building so that they can also greet visitors as they arrive for meetings. Whether over the phone or in person, the receptionist is often the first contact people have with a business—and first impressions make lasting impressions of the company.

Securities brokers spend time on the phone talking to investors and gathering information about stock offerings and other trading information. They may also provide financial counseling or help people with investment buying decisions or insurance purchases. This job requires some extensive training and, in most cases, a college degree.

The telephone company uses telephone operators to give out information and telephone numbers or to make international telephone and collect call connections.

A travel agent helps customers plan trips—either for business or for pleasure. Agents make reservations on behalf of customers with airlines, hotels, rental car agencies, tour facilities, and other places around the world. Getting a person or an organization from point A to point B can require some clever logistical maneuvering.

☞ TRY IT OUT

MAKE A PITCH
Is it time for a raise in your allowance? Or is there a special privilege you are dying to ask for but don't know what to say? Take some time to think out a polite, factual, and irresistible way to plead your cause to your parent(s). Write a script and rehearse it in front of a mirror before attempting the real thing. Good luck!

TALK IT UP

There are many organizations that would be glad to put your budding (and semiprofessional) telephone skills to work. Contact a favorite charity or nonprofit organization or a political candidate you admire. Ask if they need any help on the phones. You may have to take a training class or memorize a prepared script before making calls. This can be a great way to do some good while learning new skills.

TAKE A SURVEY

Ever wondered what all your friends think about your school? Take a survey. First, make up a list of questions to ask. Then, put together a script. Practice it and rework it until it comes across in a natural way.

Call each student in your class and ask them to complete the survey. After you've called everyone, tally up the answers and write an article for the school newspaper about the results.

 CHECK IT OUT

ON THE WEB

OVER THE TELEPHONE WIRE

If telephones are going to the tool of your trade, you might as well learn all you can about them. Here are Web sites for more information:

- ☼ Find out how telephones work at http://electronics.howstuffworks.com/telephone.htm.
- ☼ Ditto on cell phones at http://electronics.howstuffworks.com/cell-phone.htm.
- ☼ Learn more about the history of the telephone at http://www.pbs.org/wgbh/amex/telephone/index.html and http://www.att.com/attlabs/technology/forfun/alexbell and http://www.greatachievements.org/?id=2957.

📚 AT THE LIBRARY

ACTIONS SPEAK LOUDER THAN WORDS

All kinds of successful people, including telemarketers, have mastered good communication skills. Find out how to use your words and actions to find success in your life and work in books such as:

Carlson, Richard. *Don't Sweat the Small Stuff for Teens: Simple Ways to Keep Your Cool in Stressful Times.* New York: Hyperion, 2000.

Covey, Sean. *7 Habits of Highly Effective Teens.* New York: Simon and Schuster, 1998.

Fox, Janet. *Get Organized Without Losing It.* Minneapolis: Free Spirit, 2006.

Johnson, Spencer. *Who Moved My Cheese for Teens.* New York: Penguin, 2002.

McGraw, Jay. *Life Strategies for Teens.* New York: Simon and Schuster, 2000.

Ranic, Bill. *Beyond the Lemonade Stand.* New York: Razorbill, 2005.

🗣 WITH THE EXPERTS

American Teleservices Association
3815 River Crossing Parkway, Suite 20
Indianapolis, IN 46240-7756
http://www.ataconnect.org

Communication Workers of America
962 Wayne Avenue, Suite 500
Silver Spring, MD 20910-4432
http://www.cwa-union.org

Manufacturers' Agents National Association
One Spectrum Pointe, Suite 150
Lake Forest, CA 92630-2286
http://www.manaonline.org

United States Telecom Association
607 14th Street NW, Suite 400
Washington, DC 20005-2000
http://www.usta.org

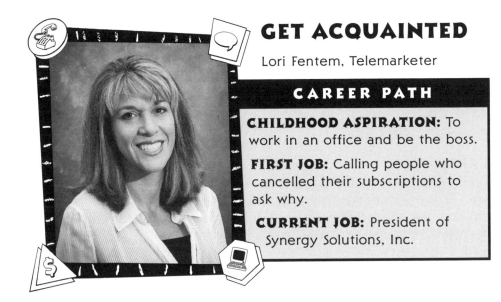

GET ACQUAINTED

Lori Fentem, Telemarketer

CAREER PATH

CHILDHOOD ASPIRATION: To work in an office and be the boss.

FIRST JOB: Calling people who cancelled their subscriptions to ask why.

CURRENT JOB: President of Synergy Solutions, Inc.

EARLY WARNING SIGNS

Lori Fentem says that it was pretty clear from an early age that she'd find success in the telemarketing industry. For one thing, she was a talker. Yakking in class was the thing most likely to get her into trouble at school. But, she soon discovered, it was also the thing that would mark a very successful career—one that began when she was only 15 years old.

That's when she started working her very first phone job. The job involved calling people to find out why they had recently cancelled their subscription to the *Chicago Tribune*. If they said it was because of crummy delivery service, her boss, a sales contractor, got credit for the subscription anyway, and Fentem's boss was very happy. Apparently, Fentem had a knack for the work because it wasn't long before she went on to do other work for her employer and ultimately was promoted to supervise an outdoor sales team of 10 people. Her team took stacks of newspapers to special events and asked people to subscribe to the paper.

The promotions kept on coming and before Fentem left to attend college in another town, she was running and training crews for both outdoor sales and the call center. All this early experience helped build Fentem's sales and leadership skills, so she was ready to try something a little different when she worked her way through college.

Her first college job required her to conduct academic research surveys over the phone. This time she just had to call people and ask them questions. With no sales quotas involved, Fentem found she could relax and enjoy what she did best—talk!

CAREER TALK

After graduating from college with a degree in sociology and urban demography, Fentem parlayed her extensive call-center experience into a full-time position at her alma mater. There she ran the university's fund-raising call center and kept busy calling former students (who by then were successfully working in various professions) to ask them for donations.

Although it's hard to imagine in today's high-tech world, Fentem says that up to that point, all her telemarketing work had been done without the help of computers. When the university decided to automate its call center, Fentem was invited to join a team of experts to put the system together from scratch. She says that this year-long project provided a great introduction to the technical side of telemarketing.

At this point, Fentem decided it was time to talk her way into a job with a little more sunshine and warm weather than central Illinois tended to offer. She landed a spot in sales with an exciting, entrepreneurial company that provided tele-marketing services on contract for other companies. There she was responsible for selling new accounts and discovered that she loved the fast-moving culture of the business world. Without all the red tape of working in a big university system, Fentem discovered that she could roll up her sleeves and make things happen.

Fentem was promoted to vice president of sales. Her company later expanded by merging with or acquiring other companies. As it kept growing, so did her career and before she knew it she was senior vice president of sales responsible for 26 call centers all over the United States and Canada.

When the company was bought out in 1999, Fentem left and, with a business partner, started her own company, Synergy Solutions, which also provides inbound and outbound teleservices on an outsourced basis to some of the largest companies in the world. Now she's responsible for things such as new business development, sales, and marketing. Working with people and lots of talking are big parts of her work these days.

THE TELEMARKETING SCENE

Fentem is first to admit that most people don't dream of growing up to have a career in telemarketing. However, she says that the industry tends to get a bad rep that it really doesn't deserve. Many people think that all telemarketers do is call and bug people to buy stuff. But Fentem says that isn't the case at all. She says that every major corporation in the world uses phones to conduct business. About 50 percent of her company's business involves providing customer support services. For instance, her employees might call senior citizens to help enroll them in necessary insurance programs or call a bank's customers to offer them a product to protect their accounts from credit theft. They might also take incoming calls for some services.

Fentem is quick to point out that telemarketing is not a dead-end job. The industry provides training, skills, and employment opportunities in safe, nontoxic work environments to all kinds of people. Entry-level positions can be ideal for students working their way through school (like Fentem did), people with disabilities, seniors, or people who need flexible, part-time hours. For those who excel in the work, there are opportunities to move up through the industry into positions of increasing responsibility and earnings. Just ask Fentem; she's made a career out of talking her way to the top.

MAKE A VERBAL DETOUR!

The preceding career highlights have introduced many fascinating options for people who love to talk. But since the general idea here is to explore all your options, here's a list of more careers. There are probably three you've never heard of before. Get acquainted with more possibilities for your future!

A WORLD OF TALKING CAREERS

IN THE PEOPLE BUSINESS

In one way or another the following careers revolve around people. Most involve using communication skills as a way to help people overcome problems and make positive changes in their lives.

adolescent-care technician
adolescent chemical-
  dependency counselor
affirmative action officer
alcohol counselor/alcoholism
  counselor
case manager
chemical dependency
  advocate/coordinator/
  technician

community activist
consumer credit counselor
corrections officer
divorce mediator
funeral director
group-home parent
home health aide
marriage counselor
psychologist
vocational counselor

TALKING MAKES THE WORLD GO ROUND

The business world revolves around effective communication skills. Find an idea that you like from the following sampling and talk your way into a good career.

advertising executive
arbitration specialist
attorney/lawyer
auctioneer
bank teller
building inspector
conference planner

consultant
consumer advocate
conference planner
editor
human-relations director
information-referral specialist

LET'S TALK ABOUT EDUCATION

When it comes right down to it, teaching anyone any skill boils down to telling what you know. These careers represent the many opportunities that are involved in educating people young and old.

admissions representative
child-care provider

coach
college professor

driving instructor
early childhood education
  specialist
interpreter
librarian

linguist
school administrator
teacher
tutor

UNCLE SAM NEEDS YOU

Government service offers a wide variety of opportunities for public servants blessed with the gift of gab. Among the opportunities are:

census worker
diplomat
military drill instructor

postal worker
public information officer

A LITTLE OF THIS, A LITTLE OF THAT

Once you start looking, you'll find opportunities for big talkers everywhere you look. There's plenty of room for having fun and lots of ways to be creative in piecing together a career that works for you. Some of these ideas provide ample room for starting out with little or no experience or advanced education and working your way up. How about waitress today and CEO of a chain of restaurants tomorrow?

bridal consultant
bus driver
car rental agent
circus ringleader
comedian
concierge
cosmetologist
cruise director
docent

entertainer
event coordinator
lifeguard
party planner
personal shopper
restaurant manager
storyteller
tour guide
waitress or waiter

DON'T STOP NOW!

GO FOR IT!

It's been a fast-paced trip so far. Take a break, regroup, and look at all the progress you've made.

1st Stop: Discover
You discovered some personal interests and natural abilities that you can start building a career around.

2nd Stop: Explore
You've explored an exciting array of career opportunities in this field. You're now aware that your career can involve either a specialized area with many educational requirements or that it may involve or a practical application of skills with a minimum of training and experience.

At this point, you've found a couple careers that make you wonder "Is this a good option for me?" Now it's time to put it all together and make an informed, intelligent choice. It's time to get a sense of what it might be like to have a job like the one(s) you're considering. In other words, it's time to move on to step three and do a little experimenting with success.

3rd Stop: Experiment

By the time you finish this section, you'll have reached one of three points in the career planning process.

1. **Green light!** You found it. No need to look any further. This is the career for you. (This may happen to a lucky few. Don't worry if it hasn't happened yet for you. This whole process is about exploring options, experimenting with ideas, and, eventually, making the best choice for you.)

2. **Yellow light!** Close but not quite. You seem to be on the right path, but you haven't nailed things down for sure. (This is where many people your age end up, and it's a good place to be. You've learned what it takes to really check things out. Hang in there. Your time will come.)

3. **Red light!** Whoa! No doubt about it, this career just isn't for you. (Congratulations! Aren't you glad you found out now and not after you'd spent four years in college preparing for this career? Your next stop: Make a U-turn and start this process over with another career.)

Here's a sneak peek at what you'll be doing in the next section.

☀ First, you'll pick a favorite career idea (or two or three).
☀ Second, you'll link up with a whole world of great information about that career on the Internet (it's easier than you think).
☀ Third, you'll snoop around the library to find answers to the top 10 things you've just got to know about your future career.
☀ Fourth, you'll either write a letter or use the Internet to request information from a professional organization associated with this career.
☀ Fifth, you'll chat on the phone to conduct an interview.

After all that, you'll (finally!) be ready to put it all together in your very own Career Ideas for Kids career profile (see page 160).

Hang on to your hats and get ready to make tracks!

#1 NARROW DOWN YOUR CHOICES

You've been introduced to quite a few talking career ideas. You may also have some ideas of your own to add. Which ones appeal to you the most?

Write your top three choices in the spaces below. (Sorry if this is starting to sound like a broken record, but if this book does not belong to you, write your responses on a separate sheet of paper.)

1. _____

2. _____

3. _____

#2 SURF THE NET

With the Internet, you have a world of information at your fingertips. The Internet has something for everyone, and it's getting easier to access all the time. An increasing number of libraries and schools are offering access to the Internet on their computers, or you may have a computer at home.

A typical career search will land everything from the latest news on developments in the field and course notes from universities to museum exhibits, interactive games, educational activities, and more. You just can't beat the timeliness or the variety of information available on the Web.

One of the easiest ways to track down this information is to use an Internet search engine, such as Yahoo! Simply type the topic you are looking for, and in a matter of seconds you'll have a list of options from around the world. For instance, if you are looking for information about companies that make candy, use the words "candy manufacturer" to start your search. It's fun to browse—you never know what you'll come up with.

Before you link up, keep in mind that many of these sites are geared toward professionals who are already working in a particular field. Some of the sites can get pretty technical. Just use the experience as a chance to nose around the field, hang out with the people who are tops in the field, and think about whether or not you'd like to be involved in a profession like that.

Specific sites to look for are the following:

Professional associations. Find out about what's happening in the field, conferences, journals, and other helpful tidbits.

Schools that specialize in this area. Many include research tools, introductory courses, and all kinds of interesting information.

Government agencies. Quite a few are going high-tech with lots of helpful resources.

Web sites hosted by experts in the field (this seems to be a popular hobby among many professionals). These Web sites are often as entertaining as they are informative.

If you're not sure where to go, just start clicking around. Sites often link to other sites. You may want to jot down notes about favorite sites. Sometimes you can even print information that isn't copyright protected; try the print option and see what happens.

Be prepared: Surfing the Internet can be an addicting habit! There is so much awesome information. It's a fun way to focus on your future.

Write the addresses of the three best Web sites that you find during your search in the space below (or on a separate sheet of paper if this book does not belong to you).

1. _____

2. _____

3. _____

#3 SNOOP AT THE LIBRARY

Take your list of favorite career ideas, a notebook, and a helpful adult with you to the library. When you get there, go to the reference section and ask the librarian to help you find books about careers. Most libraries will have at least one set

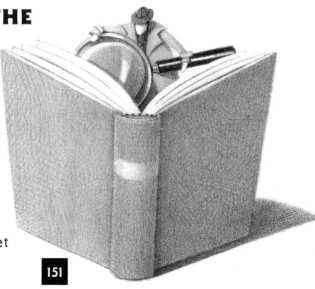

of career encyclopedias. Some of the larger libraries may also have career information on CD-ROM.

Gather all the information you can and use it to answer the following questions in your notebook about each of the careers on your list. Make sure to ask for help if you get stuck.

TOP 10 THINGS YOU NEED TO KNOW ABOUT YOUR CAREER

1. What is the purpose of this job?

2. What kind of place is this type of work usually done in? For example, would I work mostly in a busy office, outdoors, or in a laboratory?

3. What kind of time is required to do this job? For instance, is the job usually performed during regular daytime business hours or do people work various shifts around the clock?

4. What kinds of tools are used to do this job?

5. In what ways does this job involve working with other people?

6. What kind of preparation does a person need to qualify for this job?

7. What kinds of skills and abilities are needed to be successful in this type of work?

_____

8. What's a typical day on the job like?

_____

_____

9. How much money can I expect to earn as a beginner?

_____

10. What kind of classes do I need to take in high school to get ready for this type of work?

_____

#4 GET IN TOUCH WITH THE EXPERTS

One of the best places to find information about a particular career is a professional organization devoted especially to that career. After all, these organizations are full of the best and the brightest professionals working in that particular field. Who could possibly know more about how such work gets done? There are more than 450,000 organizations in the United States, so there is bound to be an association related to just about any career you can imagine.

There are several ways you can find these organizations:

1. Look at the "Check It Out—With the Experts" list following a career you found especially interesting in the Take A Trip! section of this book.

2. Go online and use your favorite search engine (such as http://www.google.com or http://yahoo.com) to find professional associations related to a career you are

interested in. You might use the name of the career, plus the words "professional association" to start your search. You're likely to find lots of useful information online, so keep looking until you hit pay dirt.

3. Go to the reference section of your public library and ask the librarian to help you find a specific type of association in a reference book called *Encyclopedia of Associations* (Farmington Hills, Mich.: Thomson Gale) Or, if your library has access to it, the librarian may suggest using an online database called *Associations Unlimited* (Farmington Hills, Mich.: Thomson Gale).

Once you've tracked down a likely source of information, there are two ways to get in touch with a professional organization.

1. Send an e-mail.

   Most organizations include a "contact us" button on their Web sites. Sometimes this e-mail is directed to a webmaster or a customer service representative. An e-mail request might look something like this:

   Subject: Request for Information
   Date: 2/1/2008 3:18:41 PM Eastern Standard Time
   From: janedoe@mycomputer.com
   To: webmaster@candyloversassociation.org

   I am a fifth-grade student, and I am interested in learning more about careers for candy lovers. Would you please send me any information you have about what people do in your industry?

   Thank you very much.
   Jane Doe

2. Write a letter requesting information.

   Your letter should be either typed on a computer or written in your best handwriting. It should include the date, the complete address of the organization you are contacting, a salutation or greeting, a brief description of your request, and a signature. Be sure to include an address where the organization can reach you with a reply. Something like the following letter would work just fine.

> Dear Sir or Madam:
>
> I am a fifth-grade student, and I would like to learn more about what it is like to work in the candy-lover profession. Would you please send me information about careers? My address is 456 Main Street, Anytown, USA 54321.
>
> Thank you very much.
>
> Sincerely,
> Jane Doe

Write the names and addresses of the professional organizations you discover on a separate sheet of paper.

#5 CHAT ON THE PHONE

Talking to a seasoned professional—someone who experiences the job day in and day out—can be a great way to get the inside story on what a career is all about. Fortunately for you, the experts in any career field can be as close as the nearest telephone.

Sure, it can be a bit scary calling up an adult whom you don't know. But two things are in your favor:

1. They can't see you. The worst thing they can do is hang up on you, so just relax and enjoy the conversation.

2. They'll probably be happy to talk to you about their job. In fact, most people will be flattered that you've called. If you happen to contact someone who seems reluctant to talk, thank them for their time and try someone else.

Here are a few pointers to help make your telephone interview a success:

☀ Mind your manners and speak clearly.
☀ Be respectful of their time and position.
☀ Be prepared with good questions and
  take notes as you talk.

One more common sense reminder: be careful about giving out your address and DO NOT arrange to meet anyone you don't know without your parents' supervision.

TRACKING DOWN CAREER EXPERTS

You might be wondering by now how to find someone to interview. Have no fear! It's easy if you're persistent. All you have to do is ask. Ask the right people and you'll have a great lead in no time.

A few of the people to ask and sources to turn to are:

Your parents. They may know someone (or know someone who knows someone) who has just the kind of job you're looking for.

Your friends and neighbors. You might be surprised to find out how many interesting jobs these people have when you start asking them what they (or their parents) do for a living.

Librarians. Since you've already figured out what kinds of companies employ people in your field of interest, the next step is to ask for information about local employers. Although it's a bit cumbersome to use, a big volume called *Contacts Influential* can provide this kind of information.

Professional associations. Call, e-mail, or write to the professional associations you discovered using the activity on page 153 and ask for recommendations.

Chambers of commerce. The local chamber of commerce probably has a directory of employers, their specialties, and their phone numbers. Call the chamber, explain what you are looking for, and give them a chance to help their future workforce.

Newspaper and magazine articles. Find an article about the subject you are interested in. Chances are pretty good that it will mention the name of at least one expert in the field. The article probably won't include the person's phone number (that would be too easy), so you'll have to look for clues. Common clues include the name of the company that they work for, the town that they live in, and, if the person is an author, the name of their publisher. Make a few phone calls and track them down (if long distance calls are involved, make sure to get your parents' permission first).

INQUIRING KIDS WANT TO KNOW

Before you make the call, make a list of questions to ask. You'll cover more ground if you focus on using the five W's (and the H) that you've probably heard about in your creative writing classes: Who? What? Where? When? How? and Why? For example:

1. Whom do you work for?

   _____

2. What is a typical workday like for you?

   _____

3. Where can I get some on-the-job experience?

   _____

4. When did you become a _____?
   (profession)

5. How much can you earn in this profession? (But remember, it's not polite to ask someone how much *he* or *she* earns.)

   _____

6. Why did you choose this profession?

   _____

Use a grid like the one below to keep track of the questions you ask in the boxes labeled "Q" and the answers you receive in the boxes labeled "A."

Who?	What?	Where?	When?	How?	Why?
Q	Q	Q	Q	Q	Q
A	A	A	A	A	A
Q	Q	Q	Q	Q	Q
A	A	A	A	A	A

One last suggestion: Add a professional (and very classy) touch to the interview process by following up with a thank-you note to the person who took time out of a busy schedule to talk with you.

#6 INFORMATION IF POWER

As you may have noticed, a similar pattern of information was used for each of the careers profiled in this book. Each entry included:

- ☼ a general description of the career
- ☼ Try It Out activities to give readers a chance to find out what it's really like to do each job
- ☼ a list of Web sites, library resources, and professional organizations to check for more information
- ☼ a get-acquainted interview with a professional

You may have also noticed that all the information you just gathered would fit rather nicely in a Career Ideas for Kids career profile of your own. Just fill in the blanks on the following pages to get your thoughts together (or, if this book does not belong to you, use a separate sheet of paper).

And by the way, this formula is one that you can use throughout your life to help you make fully informed career choices.

CAREER TITLE _____

WHAT IS A_____?

Use career encyclopedias and other resources to write a description of this
career.

SKILL SET

✔ _____
✔ _____
✔ _____

_____
_____
_____
_____

 TRY IT OUT

Write project ideas here. Ask your parents and your teacher
to come up with a plan.

_____
_____
_____
_____
_____

✔ CHECK IT OUT

🖱 ON THE WEB

List Internet addresses of interesting Web sites you find.

_____
_____
_____
_____
_____

 AT THE LIBRARY

List the titles and authors of books about this career.

_____

_____

_____

_____

WITH THE EXPERTS

List professional organizations where you can learn more about this profession.

_____

_____

_____

_____

GET ACQUAINTED

Interview a professional in the field and summarize your findings.

_____

_____

_____

_____

_____

_____

_____

WHAT'S NEXT?

Whoa, everybody! At this point, you've put in some serious miles on your career exploration journey. Before you move on, let's put things in reverse for just a sec and take another look at some of the clues you uncovered about yourself when you completed the "Discover" activities in the Get in Gear chapter on pages 7 to 26.

The following activities will help lay the clues you learned about yourself alongside the clues you learned about a favorite career idea. The comparison will help you decide if that particular career idea is a good idea for you to pursue. It doesn't matter if a certain career sounds absolutely amazing. If it doesn't honor your skills, your interests, and your values, it's not going to work for you.

The first time you looked at these activities, they were numbered one through five as "Discover" activities. This time around they are numbered in the same order but labeled "Rediscover" activities. That's not done to confuse you (sure hope it doesn't!). Instead, it's done to drive home a very important point that this is an important process you'll want to revisit time and time again as you venture throughout your career—now and later.

First, pick the one career idea that you are most interested in at this point and write its name here (or if this book doesn't belong to you, blah, blah, blah—you know the drill by now):

_____

With that idea in mind, revisit your responses to the following Get in Gear activities and complete the following:

REDISCOVER #1:
WATCH FOR SIGNS ALONG THE WAY

Based on your responses to the statements on page 8, choose which of the following road signs best describes how you feel about your career idea:

- ☀ Green light—Go! Go! Go! This career idea is a perfect fit!
- ☀ Yellow light—Proceed with caution! This career idea is a good possibility, but you're not quite sure that it's the "one" just yet.
- ☀ Stop—Hit the brakes! There's no doubt about it—this career idea is definitely not for you!

REDISCOVER #2:
RULES OF THE ROAD

Take another look at the work-values chart you made on page 16. Now use the same symbols to create a work-values chart for the career idea you are considering. After you have all the symbols in place, compare the two charts and answer these questions:

- Does your career idea's **purpose** line up with yours? Would it allow you to work in the kind of **place** you most want to work in?
- What about the **time** commitment—is it in sync with what you're hoping for?
- Does it let you work with the **tools** and the kind of **people** you most want to work with?
- And, last but not least, are you willing to do what it takes to **prepare** for a career like this?

PURPOSE	PLACE	TIME
TOOLS	**PEOPLE**	**PREPARATION**

REDISCOVER #3: DANGEROUS DETOURS

Go back to page 16 and double-check your list of 10 careers that you hope to avoid at any cost.

Is this career on that list? ____Yes ____ No

Should it be? ____Yes ____ No

REDISCOVER #4:
ULTIMATE CAREER DESTINATION

Pull out the ultimate career destination brochure you made (as described on page 17). Use a pencil to cross through every reference to "my ideal career" and replace it with the name of the career idea you are now considering.

Is the brochure still true? _____Yes _____ No

If not, what would you change on the brochure to make it true?

REDISCOVER #5:
GET SOME DIRECTION

Quick! Think fast! What is your personal Skill Set as discovered on page 26?

Write down your top three interest areas:

1. _____

2. _____

3. _____

What three interest areas are most closely associated with your career idea?

1. _____

2. _____

3. _____

Does this career's interest areas match any of yours?

_____Yes _____ No

Now the big question: Are you headed in the right direction?

If so, here are some suggestions to keep you moving ahead:

- Keep learning all you can about this career—read, surf the Web, talk to people, and so on. In other words, keep using some of the strategies you used in the Don't Stop Now chapter on pages 147 to 161 to do all you can to make a fully informed career decision.
- Work hard in school and get good grades. What you do now counts! Your performance, your behavior, your attitude—all conspire to either propel you forward or hold you back.
- Get involved in clubs and other after-school activities to further develop your interests and skills. Whether it's student government, 4-H, or sports, these kinds of activities give you a chance to try new things and gain confidence in your abilities.

If not, here are some suggestions to help you regroup:

- Read other books in the Career Ideas for Kids series to explore options associated with your other interest areas.
- Take a variety of classes in school and get involved in different kinds of after-school activities to get a better sense of what you like and what you do well.
- Talk to your school guidance counselor about taking a career assessment test to help fine-tune your focus.
- Most of all, remember that time is on your side. Use the next few years to discover more about yourself, explore your options, and experiment with what it takes to make you succeed. Keep at it and look forward to a fantastic future!

HOORAY! YOU DID IT!

This has been quite a trip. If someone tries to tell you that this process is easy, don't believe them. Figuring out what you want to do with the rest of your life is heavy stuff, and it should be. If you don't put some thought (and some sweat and hard work) into the process, you'll get stuck with whatever comes your way.

You may not have things planned to a T. Actually, it's probably better if you don't. You'll change some of your ideas as you grow and experience new things. And, you may find an interesting detour or two along the way. That's okay.

The most important thing about beginning this process now is that you've started to dream. You've discovered that you have some unique talents and abilities to share. You've become aware of some of the ways you can use them to make a living—and perhaps make a difference in the world.

Whatever you do, don't lose sight of the hopes and dreams you've discovered. You've got your entire future ahead of you. Use it wisely.

PASSPORT TO YOUR FUTURE

Getting where you want to go requires patience, focus, and lots of hard work. It also hinges on making good choices. Following is a list of some surefire ways to give yourself the best shot at a bright future. Are you up to the challenge? Can you do it? Do you dare?

Put your initials next to each item that you absolutely promise to do.

___ ☼ Do my best in every class at school
___ ☼ Take advantage of every opportunity to get a wide variety of experiences through participation in sports, after-school activities, my favorite place of worship, and my community
___ ☼ Ask my parents, teachers, or other trusted adults for help when I need it
___ ☼ Stay away from drugs, alcohol, and other bad scenes that can rob me of a future before I even get there
___ ☼ Graduate from high school

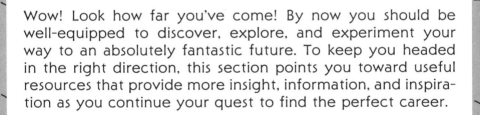

SOME FUTURE DESTINATIONS

Wow! Look how far you've come! By now you should be well-equipped to discover, explore, and experiment your way to an absolutely fantastic future. To keep you headed in the right direction, this section points you toward useful resources that provide more insight, information, and inspiration as you continue your quest to find the perfect career.

IT'S NOT JUST FOR NERDS

The school counselor's office is not just a place where teachers send troublemakers. One of its main purposes is to help students like you make the most of your educational opportunities. Most schools will have a number of useful resources, including career assessment tools (ask about the Self-Directed Search Career Explorer or the COPS Interest

Inventory—these are especially useful assessments for people your age). They may also have a stash of books, videos, and other helpful materials.

Make sure no one's looking and sneak into your school counseling office to get some expert advice!

AWESOME INTERNET CAREER RESOURCES

Your parents will be green with envy when they see all the career planning resources you have at your fingertips. Get ready to hear them whine, "But they didn't have all this stuff when I was a kid." Make the most of these cyberspace opportunities.

☀ **Adventures in Education**
http://adventuresineducation.org/middleschool
Here you'll find some useful tools to make the most of your education—starting now. Make sure to watch "The Great College Mystery," an online animation featuring Dr. Ed.

☀ **America's Career InfoNet**
http://www.acinet.org
Career sites don't get any bigger than this one! Compliments of the U.S. Department of Labor, and a chunk of your parent's tax dollars, you'll find all kinds of information about what people do, how much money they make, and where they work. Although it's mostly geared toward adults, you may want to take a look at some of the videos (the site has links to more than 450!) that show people at work.

☀ **ASVAB Career Exploration Program**
http://www.asvabprogram.com
This site may prove especially useful as you continue to think through various options. It includes sections

for students to learn about themselves, to explore careers, and to plan for their futures.

☼ Career Voyages
http://www.careervoyages.gov
This site will be especially helpful to you as you get a little older. It offers four paths to get you started: "Where do I start?" "Which industries are growing?" "How do I qualify and get a job?" and "Does education pay? How do I pay?" However, it also includes a special section especially for elementary school students. Just click the button that says "Still in elementary school?" or go to http://www.careervoyages. gov/students-elementary.cfm.

☼ Job Profiles
http://jobprofiles.org
This site presents the personal side of work with profiles of people working in jobs associated with agriculture and nature, arts and sports, business and communications, construction and manufacturing, education and science, government, health and social services, retail and wholesale, and other industries.

☼ Major and Careers Central
http://www.collegeboard.com/csearch/majors_careers
This site is hosted by the College Board (the organization responsible for a very important test called the SAT, which you're likely to encounter if you plan to go to college). It includes helpful information about how different kinds of subjects you can study in college can prepare you for specific types of jobs.

☼ Mapping Your Future
http://mapping-your-future.org/MHSS

This site provides strategies and resources for students as they progress through middle school and high school.

☼ My Cool Career
http://www.mycoolcareer.com
This site is where you can take free online self-assessment quizzes, explore your dreams, and listen to people with interesting jobs talk about their work.

☼ O*NET Online
http://online.onetcenter.org
This U.S. Department of Labor site provides comprehensive information about hundreds of important occupations. Although you may need to ask a parent or teacher to help you figure out how to use the system, it can be a good source of digging for nitty-gritty details about a specific type of job. For instance, each profile includes a description of the skills, abilities, and special knowledge needed to perform each job.

☼ Think College Early
http://www.ed.gov/students/prep/college/
thinkcollege/early/edlite-tcehome.html
Even though you almost need a college degree just to type the Web address for this U.S. Department of Education site, it contains some really cool career information and helps you think about how college might fit into your future plans.

☼ What Interests You?
http://www.bls.gov/k12
This Bureau of Labor Statistics site is geared toward students. It lets you explore careers by interests such as reading, building and fixing things, managing money, helping people, and more.

JOIN THE CLUB!

Once you've completed eighth grade, you are eligible to check out local opportunities to participate in Learning for Life's career education programs. Some communities offer Explorer posts that sponsor activities with students interested in industries that include the arts and humanities, aviation, business, communications, engineering, fire service, health, law enforcement, law and government, science, skilled trades, or social services. To find a local office, go to http://www.learning-for-life.org/exploring/main.html and type your zip code.

Until then, you can go online and play *Life Choices*, a really fun and challenging game where you get one of five virtual jobs at http://www.learning-for-life.org/games/LCSH/index.html.

MORE CAREER BOOKS ESPECIALLY FOR KIDS

It's especially important that people your age find out all they can about as many different careers as they can. Books like the ones listed below can introduce all kinds of interesting ideas that you might not encounter in your everyday life.

Greenfeld, Barbara C., and Robert A. Weinstein. *The Kids' College Almanac: A First Look at College.* 3d ed. Indianapolis, Ind.: JIST Works, 2005.
Young Person's Occupational Outlook Handbook. 6th ed. Indianapolis, Ind.: JIST Works, 2006.

Following are brief descriptions of several series of books geared especially toward kids like you. To find copies of these books, ask your school or public librarian to help you search the library computer system using the name of the series.

SOME FUTURE DESTINATIONS

Career Connections (published by UXL)
This extensive series features information and illustrations
about jobs for people interested in art and design, entrepre-
neurship, food, government and law, history, math and computers, and the performing arts as well as those who want to
work with their hands or with living things.

Career Ideas for Kids (written by Diane Lindsey Reeves, published by Ferguson)
This series of interactive career exploration books features 10
different titles for kids who like adventure and travel, animals
and nature, art, computers, math and money, music and
dance, science, sports, talking, and writing.

Careers Without College (published by Peterson's)
These books offer a look at options available to those who
prefer to find jobs that do not require a college degree and
include titles focusing on cars, computers, fashion, fitness,
health care, and music.

Cool Careers (published by Rosen Publishing)
Each title in this series focuses on a cutting-edge occupation
such as computer animator, hardware engineer, multimedia
and new media developer, video game designer, Web entre-
preneur, and webmaster.

Discovering Careers for Your Future (published by Ferguson)
This series includes a wide range of titles that focus on adventure, art, construction, fashion, film, history, nature, publishing, and radio and television.

Risky Business (written by Keith Elliot Greenberg, published by
Blackbirch Press)
These books feature stories about people with adventurous
types of jobs and include titles about a bomb squad officer,
disease detective, marine biologist, photojournalist, rodeo
clown, smoke jumper, storm chaser, stunt woman, test pilot,
and wildlife special agent.

HEAVY-DUTY RESOURCES

Career encyclopedias provide general information about a lot of professions and can be a great place to start a career search. Those listed here are easy to use and provide useful information about nearly a zillion different jobs. Look for them in the reference section of your local library.

Career Discovery Encyclopedia, 6th ed. New York: Ferguson, 2006.

Careers for the 21st Century. Farmington Hills, Mich.: Lucent Books, 2002.

Children's Dictionary of Occupations. Princeton, N.J.: Cambridge Educational, 2004.

Encyclopedia of Career and Vocational Guidance. New York: Ferguson, 2005.

Farr, Michael, and Laurence Shatkin. *Enhanced Occupational Outlook Handbook*. 6th ed. Indianapolis, Ind.: JIST Works, 2006.

Occupational Outlook Handbook. Washington, D.C.: U.S. Government Printing Office, 2006.

FINDING PLACES TO WORK

Even though you probably aren't quite yet in the market for a real job, you can learn a lot about the kinds of jobs you might find if you were looking by visiting some of the most popular job-hunting sites on the Internet. Two particularly good ones to investigate are America's Job Bank (http://www.ajb.org) and Monster (http://www.monster.com).

INDEX

Page numbers in **boldface** indicate main articles. Page numbers in *italics* indicate photographs.